Photo by Judy Brown

FROM ALLEN GINSBERG'S INTRODUCTION:

Plymell and his friends inventing the Wichita *Vortex* contribute to a tradition stretching back from Lamantia thru Sherwood Anderson to Poe and earlier American vibration artists . . . . The *Vortex* vibration is in these Apocalypse Rose writings — unearthly hum of a tornado of consciousness droning in on a brain born to provincial solitude, perverted local politics, sick police . . . blackout of Whitman's blissful Adhesiveness among Citizens . . . . I interpret his statement as prophetic fragment memory of innocence, visionary great fear, & Warm glimmer: a new species?

$1.60   Dave Haselwood Books   San Francisco

HAND ON THE DOORKNOB

Birthplace of Charles Plymell in Holcomb, Kansas.
Charles in doorway with sisters during the flood, 1939.

*"By 1935, my father had sold his part of the ranch
and took his family to Holcomb, Kansas, where I was born
in a converted chicken shed built to protect us from the
black dust storms that had long covered the once-thriving
stage lines a few miles away."*

HAND ON THE DOORKNOB

A CHARLES PLYMELL READER

EDITED BY

DAVID BREITHAUPT

WATER ROW PRESS
SUDBURY
2000

Grateful acknowledgment is given to the editors and publishers of all the periodicals and books in which some of this
material has previously been published.

Water Row Press
P O Box 438
Sudbury MA 01776
email waterrow@aol.com
www.waterrowbooks.com
write for a free catalogue

Library of Congress Cataloging-in-Publication Data

Plymell, Charles
      Hand on the doorknob — a Charles Plymell reader /
edited by David Breithaupt.

         p. cm.

      ISBN 0-934953-63-5. — ISBN 0-934953-59-7 (pbk.)
      I. Breithaupt, Davd.   II. Title.
PS3566.L95A6   1999   98-54825
811'.54—dc21   CIP

Cover by Bruce Hilvitz
Pre-press guru: Henri Hadida at Pride Printing
Printed in USA
Book design and typsetting by Pamela Beach Plymell

Charles and Pam Plymell, Eiffel Tower, Paris, 1968

Dedicated to
Pam
for her tireless work
and
to Billy and Elizabeth
for being strong

SOME MINOR RAMBLINGS FROM THE EDITOR

When I was a kid, my older brothers and I would gather our resources (mostly financial and scientific), and create the greenish concoction commonly known as gunpowder. All we needed was a little salt peter, some charcoal and sulfur, a little luck in mixing the right proportions and voila! We were set.

This act of creation led us to days and nights of endless activity. Old Coke bottles were filled with our special recipe, lit, and exploded in the night. The bottle would shoot streaks of flame and sparks into the air and implode with a crazy boom. Amazing and wonderfully Freudian. We'd scrawl weird designs on the ground with our mixture, creating flaming crazy eights or emblazoning our favorite forbidden words. This was so much fun, so incredibly easy, I wondered, why isn't everybody doing this?

I think of those gunpowder days and nights every time I pick up a piece of writing by Charles Plymell. Why isn't everybody reading this guy? Granted, some of his early books are out-of-print and fall into the pricey category of collectable books, but others are new or have been reprinted, and thus are readily available and affordable (there are also institutions known as libraries which lend you books free of charge!) So many times his name comes up on the lips of his famous contemporaries. Yet, when I told my friends that I had the good fortune to be editing a book of collected works by none other than the Charles Plymell, the response was too frequently, who?

Well, enough of that. Let us hope that this book gives Charles Plymell his proper laurels. I have tried to assemble a representative collection of Plymell's work, ranging from his early *Journals From Lysidia 1962*, and *Apocalypse Rose* (which prompted Allen Ginsberg to muse, "a new species?"), to his more recent short fiction and memoir pieces including Eating and Drinking with the Beats. I also could not leave out Plymell's Curled in Character, his remembrance of cartoonists past. Curled recalls the beginning of Zap Comix which Plymell helped launch on his very own printing press. Zap became a household name in every underground home, kick starting the careers of such artists as Robert Crumb and S. Clay Wilson.

Whatever you're looking for, it's in here somewhere, be it in the poems, memoirs or short stories. Here is the man who rode with Neal Cassady, fished with William S. Burroughs, and wrote all along the way, his ear straining toward the Vortex. Read on, it's more fun than gunpowder.

David Breithaupt
Gambier, Ohio

AUTHOR'S PREFACE

In the absence of ethnicities to help establish my formative identity (I was, actually without people for miles around, two persons for each square mile, demographically) the Psychic Trauma of Time, in the sense of singularity, was one of my most impressionistic sensations alone in the wind tunes under what seemed cosmic-sky-shivering-sun vibrations. I still get the sensation when I ride my bike down the blacktop highway on a clear sunny day, that I am in Kansas, "gypping" school, riding down the road glistening and shimmering in the translucent and transcendental warm vibrations.

"Singularity" is a term used by physicists. For me, it is strong feeling that evokes the "who am I" "someday I won't be here." Some presume an answer in death, or why else would they commit suicide. To stop the question, no doubt. The personal emotions set off by this awareness, however "unaware" probably vary greatly throughout the human population. In my personal philosophy, I believe one can be shocked by it, traumatized by the big question. I believe the cause of criminality lies in one's own fear of the unknown. This might make a good case for cloning... erasing the enigma...so to speak. A sub-emotional benefit also might be in making the most desired beauty available to all...anyway, cloning is an instinctive human imperative that probably cannot be stopped.

Aesthetics have always been a part of my life. I became interested in poetry through beauty. The beauty of words and images gave me a feeling not unlike the earlier described shivering in the cosmic sun. Like Rimbaud, I understood little poetry, and to this day, I am baffled by most of the poetry I read in the mainstream. I spent much of my life teaching in English departments fretting about the direction of linguistics, rhetoric, poetry, newspeak, etc. Poetry, a private aesthetic, is made with the most common elements—words. A future in high words is always problematic.

My nationalism and chauvinism were very simply felt in the song, "I'm from Kansas, dear old Kansas/ the land of sunflowers and wheat..." I stood on the "far off hill" in a later stanza of the song; indeed later, on the "far-out hill." I did not belong to anything or anyone. I had no affiliations then, and I have none, now. Ditto for the church. Orthodoxies, like political systems, to me are tiresome games. They can even befuddle the best minds of a generation. There is an innate, perhaps a national expectation...to "belong." I will say only that I believe in Belief. Systems and labels are appealing to human nature. It is much easier to belong than to not.

My family situation left me on my own. I dropped out of my freshman year of high school; I became a 50's rebel and later a hipster involved in a subculture of the early 50's was that of hot rods, Fords, and drive-ins. Kansas City to Los Angeles was my geography. I worked in the Northwest and in the Arizona desert. I had spent my youth on a farm on the high plains of Kansas. Later I gravitated to a cooler lifestyle of a hipster hanging around that old bebop saxtown, Kansas City. I saw famous names in race music and R&B who came to play in dives across the tracks in Wichita. I could go to the honky-tonks and hear all the famous country artists and score sweetheart bennies from a back up band member who carried them in quart Mason jars.

A great deal of my poetry has to do with generations, fads, and lifestyles. My K.C. to L.A. early years were recalled and written about later. I didn't do much at Wichita University. I was the typical creative jerk who stuffed my own poems (not very good ones) in the campus literary magazine. Much of it was trite textbooky stuff from the canons of English departments in those days. An art professor gave me a copy of

Howl. This was in the mid-to-late 50's. Rebel, hipster, to art student. That sounds about right. The artist, Bob Branaman, who was in the Wichita City Jail with me, talked of enrolling in college when he returned from the "P Farm".

I took another trip to San Francisco in 1962; my sister, Betty, was living there. I stayed with some friends who had moved from Wichita to a house on Ashbury St. next to the corner one that faced Haight St. Soon I would sit in a head shop in the lower Haight with Richard Brautigan watching the scene unfold. San Francisco Bay Area was the right time and place for the psychedelic revolution.

I moved out of the Haight into "The Gough Street Pad" or "End Pad" as Glenn Todd called it. He recently found a piece he had written in 1963 describing the party where the Beats meet the vortex at the Gough St. Pad. I lived there afterwards with Neal and Allen. I had met Neal previously. This was the first time I met Allen. My first impression was that he came to make history. The sense of making history had a effect on my own experimental writing.

The poetry in this book is written for the most part in and after the 60's to the present. The autobiographical substance remembering the 50's was written after I had met the Beats. Before that, I was living a parallel lifestyle as the Beats—the generic "Hip" as in Lord Buckley influenced the Beats. I wasn't writing in the 50's; seriously writing, like they were. I didn't become serious about my writing until I had been published in *Evergreen Review* and other noteworthy and lucrative places.

I had printed some S. Clay Wilson drawings while we were in Lawrence, Kansas. Later Pam and I had an old Multilith in our apartment in S.F. We printed the first Robert Crumb *ZAP*. I worked on the S.F. docks for a while until an emissary came to ask me to come to The Johns Hopkins Writing Seminars. Pam and I developed a strong connection to Baltimore. Our daughter was born there. We met a friend who helped launch the *Coldspring Journal*. We were visited there by several poets and read poetry there. Baltimore is a very ethnic city, and I enjoyed being around many different people.

I had just enough pretense to teach in college, and I was associated with the Beat Generation. City Lights published my first book. The seeds of nostalgia are fondness. I can get a nostalgic buzz for at least three generations I was fond of. Though my work has also been labeled as an outsider, or outlaw, or proletariat, or part of the Invisible generation of Hugh Fox, I became closer to some of the Beats, lost track of some, and remained cordial to those with whom I had differences, but my work has remained associated with them, at least as a post-beat. As a cool street kid in the 50's, I would never have guessed I would be sitting with another Adjunct Professor, Allen Ginsberg, eating dinner for the last time with Mr. Burroughs in Kansas.

The loss of so many Beats in the span of a year or so left a very hollow feeling in me. From a selfish point of view, I saw them as the last line of defense. If things started going wrong, I could depend on them for a voice of sanity as far as seeing the truth and making an honest statement. If the establishment came down wrong, it was good to have the public audience the Beats commanded. They were my authority and spokesmen on issues of state and Literature, especially in freedom of speech. I hate to lose that security, especially at my age, which brings me to the front lines, now. New linguistic expressions are being charged with spirit in this age of Apostasy; the art of poetry has fallen into Babel. There may be an end to art and I may have to wait in line for training from the National Poetry Program to compete in slam performances.

Well, here's to further!

Charles Plymell
Cherry Valley, New York
February 2000

ESSAYS

Letter to Hamley & Company, October 1942,
written by Charles Plymell, age 7, Ulysses, Kansas.

John Norton (back to camera), Elizabeth Plymell,
Pamela Plymell, Allen Ginsberg, Janine Pommy-Vega.
Plymell house, Cherry Valley, 1970s.

EATING AND DRINKING WITH THE BEATS

After the famous Gough St. bash where the Beats met the Hippies, Allen invited me over for a light dinner. He was just back from India trying to get Neal settled in, and Peter, and Anne. They later shared the Gough St. flat with me. Allen was staying with his old friend from the beat days, "Dr. Radar", who lived just down the hill from Ferlinghetti. A few days earlier we had visited Larry at his house, ate some salad Larry made, and some cheese and wine. Larry liked good French wine. Radar had a monkey in his yard. Allen said I had to go through the "Monkey Test," whatever that was. He told me it would bite if it sensed the wrong aura. I passed the test. Allen had gone shopping in North Beach with Larry and had bought some caviar, wine, fruit and cheese. He asked me if I liked caviar. I didn't. He had some dark bread to put it on. We pieced around and drank some wine and rolled a joint. He told me about his Indian travels and asked me about McClure and some other poets from Kansas. Peter came to the door and walked right past the monkey. Allen said he would come over to the Gough St. flat and bring some poems for a little mag I was doing, called "Now." Both Mike and Allen had written a poem to each other, a kind of apology to each other to set the tone for the new "love" generation. Bruce Conners, an artist from Wichita, would soon paint LOVE in street lettering in the lane where Oak St. turned onto the freeway. I formed my lasting impression of Allen Ginsberg: He came to make history.

Thanksgiving dinner at 1403 Gough St., 1963 just after the Kennedy assassination when Robert LaVigne dropped by, talked to Ginsberg, who was tidying up the kitchen. Robert spotted dirt on the floor and wiped it clean, making a point to Allen, who had lived in the flat in the 50's and had taken Robert's love, Peter. Later that day was the big dinner in the dining room. Neal Cassady was rolling a joint from his shoe box lid, telling stories, while Anne and others were planning the traditional Thanksgiving meal. As the day grew late, several others confounded the cooking. Old Frank, my sister Betty's husband, who got me a job on the docks, was telling his stories of the wild early west about his being the offspring of the Sheriff of Deadwood, South Dakota and a Black madam. The scene was somewhat gloomy, as it had been overcast for several days, but still pleasant and traditionally reverent. Someone off the street had happened by and was included in the meal. There were lots of drinks and Peter Orlovsky insisted on doing the dishes; he obsessively washed everything.

It was at "Foster Fudds" (Foster's cafeteria) just below the Hotel Wentley the same year when I grabbed a naked lunch with Ginsberg and Leary before going to a party. The talk was serious, concerning contraband and the law. Leary had just come from Big Sur where he visited Bob Branaman, who had cooked him a Kansas stew.

At Mike's Pool Hall in North Beach Pam and I ate fantastic minestrone. The salami factory was next door with salami sandwiches on sourdough bread. Pam was 17 years old, so I had to sneak her in. In those days, the old Italian men sat at the checkered table cloths and played Caruso on the juke box as they studied the pool players. Pam and I then went over to City Light's basement to look over a manuscript Ferlinghetti was going to publish. Later I joined Whalen and Ginsberg for a photo in what was to become Kerouac Alley.

Allen, Neal, Anne and I had planned a trip to Bolinas to see another friend of mine from Lawrence, Karen Wright, who had visited Gough St. to play Dylan's "Blowing in the Wind" for us for the first time. Neal had been fighting with Anne and jumped in his '39 Pontiac ready to drive. As we rounded the coastal hills and curves, Neal began gearing down the car with the stick shift hitting second gear to slow down while pulling the emergency brake (as it was called in those days) with one hand and slapping Anne with the other. He informed us that the brakes on the car were out. Allen prudently advised him to slow down, but this made him drive faster. Allen and I were being tossed around in the back seat like two Marx Brothers extras. Allen managed to get out his camera and took the famous photo of Neal, eyes off the road, head turned to Anne, cursing: the shot with the torn headliner of the Pontiac above Neal. We stopped at a snack shop where I snapped a photo. Neal liked junk food because he usually wasn't "meal hungry" on speed. When we arrived, Neal spotted a copy of *On The Road* and a comfortable chair and began reading dramatically. Karen fixed a Guacamole dip and Mexican dinner using just ripe black Avocados from the lower San Joaquin.

In 1966, Allen Ginsberg came to Wichita in his VW camper, Peter driving and taking care of brother Julius. I told them to meet me downtown at the crossroad of America, at Main and Douglas where 50's hoodlum hipsters used to score criss-cross Benzedrine and lounge-lizards bopped the night train in. By the time I arrived, Allen and Peter had found metropolitanism at the Chinese restaurant where petty gangsters hung out. Allen was delighted to walk down old cowtown streets past the pawnshops, barbecue joints, R&B race music dives and cowboy honky-tonks. We spent hours drinking at Okie's bar, swilling up the 3.2 beer and blues. Orlovsky sang and drank and yodeled. He was very much into real tear-jerker hillbilly pathos. We went to Chances R where Glenn Todd recorded a scene from a visit in '63 in a story he wrote at the time and later found. I've included a section from it in his postscript.

Robert Frank and his film assistant landed at the Wichita airport. Next to Okie's bar was the seedy old Hotel Eaton with a stained decor of decadent elegance, which remains to this day as it turned into a elegant flophouse for the poor. Robert took photos of the large oil painting of Carry Nation above a bar she had axed. Past the marbled registry was an attended elevator and a sleepy elevator operator. The elevator has old folding-caged doors. Beyond it were the urinals and marbled sinks. Next to that was the "all night long" cafe where dejected hillbillies and old blues sax players ate. It is written about in Pat O'Connor's, "Moody's Skidrow Beanery." Here you could get chops and even chicken-fried steak, an awful Kansas favorite of the old timers. To us, the greatest thing on the menu was a real Kansas breakfast, from biscuits to steaks and pancakes with eggs on top of them, bacon, home fries peppered and catsupped. It was a good "wee hours" breakfast place after one had been drunk and back again halfway sober and tingly but tired from hangin' an' bangin' one's chops and thighs all night long.

Summer 1967, Pam and I, Janine Pommy Vega and Herbert Huncke stopped in a diner on the way to the clinic in Northern California where Jerry Garcia later died; we were to take Huncke there to clean up. At the diner Huncke ordered pancakes and poured a lot of junk-sick syrup on them. He then looked blank, went on the nod as his face fell into the plate of pancakes. He recovered, looked at the waitress and the customers and said. "I bet you all think I'm crazy. Well I am!"

It was a year later when Robert Crumb moved to San Francisco and Don Donahue came over to our flat on Post St. where Pam and I had an antique Multilith. I showed Don how Robert would have to draw color overlays for us to print the color cover of the original ZAP. The pages were designed to do the maximum size for the old Multi and were printed on newsprint. There were many copies destroyed in the printing, adding perhaps to its thousands of dollars value at Sotheby's decades later. That night we went to Crumb's apartment to collate the comix, where his wife, Dana, later the cookbook author, made us a Crumb cake with a cartoon icing.

By 1968, Pam and I were in London and visited Burroughs at his 8 Duke Street flat. He had written me a cut up of some poems of mine and others in the second issue of *Now*, titled *Now Now* with lettering by Branaman of bodies in sex. I wrote the following poem:

8 DUKE ST., LONDON, 1968

In London in a very neat
and sensible flat,
lives the genius
of contemporary American prose.

More like a poet
he veers and speaks both
naturally and subliminally.
More like a medium
he chats pleasantly
from a space apart
or from a chamber
of spirits disguised
in an everyday world.

A tall man, slightly stooped
from the weight of all
combinations and formulas
of all possible plots,

Mr. Burroughs rises
and leans against the window ledge
…could have been a St. Louis
merchant or farmer
about to speculate on the weather.

"Those birds," he says, gesturing out
the window to a flock that caught his fancy:
"in the mornings they fly one way
and in the evenings they
fly back the other way."

And with that he reached for his hat
and we went to the local pub for brandy.

End of the summer of '68, Pam and I met Allen in NYC
and went with him to the William F. Buckley show, "Firing
Line." Ed Sanders and Jack Kerouac met us there. Kerouac
was doing a show with Buckley as two Republicans discussing
the Viet Nam War. Kerouac said it was a conspiracy between
the North and South Vietnamese to get more American Jeeps
over there. He then made some remarks about Jews referring
to Ginsberg in the audience. As we left, I was behind Kerouac
walking past Truman Capote's dressing room door, opened
for trolling. Someone said there's Truman Capote. Kerouac
turned around saying "Where is that little queer, I've been
wanting to......." At that point a crowd gathered in his dressing
room and the encounter ended amicably, if not humorously.
As we went down the stairs, Kerouac grabbed me by the col-
lar and said something like "who do you think you are...?" I
shoved him against the wall and said something about the

same. Allen acted typically, both woeful and excited by the action. We then went to a nearby bar and sat for a long while, Jack drinking hard liquor, sitting next to Allen and Pam, animated, talking seriously about things I don't recall. I sat in the booth on the other side of the table with two men who were with Kerouac, not saying much, eating fries and drinking beer. Later I learned that this was the last time Allen and Jack saw each other.

We were on our way to Cherry Valley with Allen and stopped at the Big Pink's House where they were assembling for a Jam. It was a big pink suburban-type ranch house. I wrote the following poem:

AT THE BIG PINK'S HOUSE

They came from the city,
from the hills around
Pittsburgh... Amarillo.
One packed a lunch
drove a Hudson Hornet
and the music sure was good.

The house had vinyl pink siding,
big front room for the band.
The women made lunch.
We ate near a large rock,
drinking good scotch,
enjoying mystic truth's smooch
the music sure was good.

A subtle smoke beyond the brain
invoked an Indian ghost over the lake
and floated into the rising full moon.

That night we left with bard and harmonium
drove to Cherry Valley and Kansas across states
that didn't matter anymore on to San Francisco.

We stayed at Allen's farm in Cherry Valley and ate borsch and fresh vegetable dinner made from some of the vegetables Peter had brought in from the garden. To entertain Elizabeth, Allen played some of his Blake songs on his antique organ.

In the bucolic hills of Cherry Valley, Reality Sandwiches and Kaddish were being translated into French by Mary Beach and Claude Pélieu. There were many transients staying at the poor little isolated farmhouse, so cooking outside was helpful. Usually the fare was whatever anyone thoughtful happened to bring from town. The cooking was primitive and sanitary conditions didn't prevail. The water source was below the cabin and an outhouse was uphill. Expensive cookware was abundant, however, as were many anachronisms at the farm. Most were alleged vegetarians or had haphazard new-aged diets; although, it was rumored that Peter ate steak on the sly when he made trips to town. He had a pet pig, which grew to 600 lbs. and shared Peter's bed when the weather was cold. When Peter left the farm, he gave the pig to someone on condition that it wouldn't be eaten. It wasn't long before someone said it had been hit by a car. Things weren't always as reverent as the setting. Corso and Orlovsky were always fighting, mainly because Corso wanted to roast the pig, and Pelieu was talking about everyone in disdain and disgust, especially when they were naked in the pond, calling Corso "Zucchini Face" and the like. Claude and Mary did "miraculously" transform some garden vegetables into a great French vinaigrette salad that Allen exclaimed as the best he had eaten and why couldn't Peter do that, etc.

In 1975, James Grauerholtz, John Giorno, and William Burroughs came to dinner at our house in Cherry Valley, which is now the "Rose and Kettle Restaurant." Pam had gone

out of her way to fix Texas Barbeque Ribs, for Bill's recollec-
tions of his Texas "farming days." She had to special order the
long ribs because we couldn't buy them in Yankee country. I
hand made potato chips, slicing each one keenly with a
butcher knife at Bill's interest. We had Vodka for him, of
course and the rest of us drank Carlsberg's Elephant Ale, a
favorite of mine. Orlovsky came down from the East Hill
"Committee on Poetry" farm to eat with us. He was lamenting
one of his Guru's ill health, and pressed Bill for his feelings.
Burroughs snarled, "I don't give a shit if he lives or dies!" Later
Burroughs prowled the house selecting a bedroom, checking
out my empty Percodan bottle, placing it back on the shelf
with a Hmmph! The next day we went up to the farm's pond
and Peter stripped and jumped in to exhibit a Tarzan swim.

Sometime later, Janine Pommy Vega and Allen came to
dinner at the same place, Allen in his farmer's overalls. We
had a big garden and our daughter, Elizabeth helped us gather the vegetables.

Gerard Malanga came to dinner and showed Pam how to
make a vinaigrette, which she still makes for salads. Carl
Solomon and Ray Bremser used to sit on the porch and watch
the action downtown Cherry Valley and tell fishing stories. Ray
and I made our daily trips to the local drugstore and then to
Cooperstown to get our daily bottles of Turpin Hydrate and
Codeine and a six-pack of cheap beer for Ray.

During that time I went with Anne Waldman, Ginsberg
and Burroughs to Montreal for a "counterculture" reading at
the Bibliotèque Nationale. Bill started with cocktails, not wanting to eat heavy before going on stage. He ordered a Vodka,
and I, never knowing quite what to drink, ordered the same.
He quickly changed his order. After dinner was served, Allen

ordered a glass of milk. Burroughs angrily reprimanded him for it and said he shouldn't have that; it would fuck up his vocal chords on stage. We met Mary Beach and Claude Pelieu there. Claude immediately made enemies refusing to speak French. The organizers had pegged him as a CIA agent. The whole reading turned into a farce, Allen and Anne putting the best face on it. Allen visited with Emmett Grogan. Claude saw all of the "counterculture" as bullshit and put down the Quebecquois. I hopped a bus and returned to Cherry Valley writing the following poem:

OH BONY ROBOT DRIVER

Take me to the hard jackpot
To the vacant house, the hill and the riverbank
Then pour some gravity
On the wheels to
Just glide around the corners.
I got way down blue inside
that day,
drove west out of Albany...
Toward a stretch of valleys
and high hills.

Like in the western states
that scarred their sunsets in me
many times before,
bottle at my feet,
red dirt canyon rim.

Back home the cold mountain hangs still.
I slipped into my longjohns,
put on my earphones
lay back in a foam rubber flight.
Put on a record of Hank Williams' blues
Confessed to a tune I didn't want to hear.

And I didn't know
where the magnetized needle

would take the full moon
burning outside my window.
Maybe a slight reading of biorhythms
would produce a flight pattern
into that milkweed sleeve
the crimson sunset lined against the space where I
could not aim my gliding flocks of memory . . . .

Pam, Elizabeth and I went on vacation to the city. Burroughs graciously gave us his loft below Centre St. in the financial district while he and James went abroad. There was a grand (old) piano. Patti Smith called him daily on his answering machine. Upon their return, James fixed us a light dinner and Bill downed a few glasses of Vodka.

Through Elliott Coleman at Hopkins, we got Allen the F. Scott Fitzgerald room across from the Homewood Campus for a few days. We had moved back to Baltimore. We had Allen for dinner at our place there for a few meals and then helped him find a room at the Albion Hotel, where he studied Blake for a week or so. Near the Albion Hotel was a coffee shop that served a Baltimore oddity: A hot dog rolled up in a slice of baloney and slice of Velveeta cheese baked all hot and greasy on a bun. I mentioned it years later, thinking I imagined it, to Roxie Powell, who worked at the Mayor's office nearby. He said he loved them and ate them all the time. We fared better during crab season when Robert Bly visited us. I was teaching at St. Mary's College in Maryland, and we had fresh crab catch.

After my book signing party at the Gotham for Trashing of America, the Hornicks took Pam, me, Mary, Claude, and Jean-Louis Brau to a very expensive Italian restaurant where I had "Hay and Straw" at about a hundred dollars a plate. Jean-

Louis was talking about his "Situationist Party" in France. Our hosts seemed shocked to be in the presence of real revolutionaries. We got stinking drunk and in the restroom Claude and Jean-Louis started spewing ethnic slurs. I repeated them at the table, which included Allen. Lita Hornick said she had never witness such behavior "since Leroy Jones". She never spoke to me again.

We had moved to another house in Cherry Valley by the time Allen brought his stepmother to lunch with us at the notorious "Bowling Alley" in Cherry Valley where the waitresses slung burnt toast and would say, amicably, that if we didn't like it, to fix it ourselves. As on many occasions, Allen stopped at our house for soup or whatever Pam was fixing. Allen knew good soup and knew Pam's cooking, but one time his veggie driver embarrassed him by declining because it was made with chicken broth. Pam brought the driver a plate of veggie compost.

Burroughs assigned to Huncke the gift of ferreting. In one of Huncke's visits to us in Baltimore, we took him to the train station. He was ever so polite and tight and had given an incredible reading with me and Bremser at an all-night dopester bar. He spotted a fancy diner and said it looked "Right." We all ordered hamburgers, french fries and coffee. The coffee and fries were all right. The hamburger was more than right. Just the right amount of leftover grease slightly grilled on generous buns. The hamburger had been hand pattied cooked to order. Thin slices of onion, tomatoes, pickles with the letttuce to the side unwilted. We were high, of course, and ate the American icon with relish.

James Grauerholtz had invited me to read in Lawrence. My son, Billy and I were visiting Kansas, my home state and on to Wichita from Lawrence. Rob Melton at K.U. had scored us a place to stay on campus. I had my mother's pump 22 rifle with us that she had used to feed us kids jackrabbits (Hoover Steaks) during the Great Depression. James fixed us a good sirloin and said to bring the rifle over, that Bill would want to see it. Bill balanced it on one finger remarking how well it was made saying, "They don't make 'em like this anymore. Feel it Charley, just like a woman's leg!" He aimed it around the house and pumped it and pulled the trigger. He then got out his loaded 38 Special and slapped it in my hand. "Feel this," he said, "It'll stop anyone in their tracks." He got out his collection of knives to show Billy and me, having a story for each one. We looked over the knifes some more while James fixed dinner. Bill rolled a joint and passed it to me. I had an article I was reading about the hallucinogenic properties under a frog's skin that had been found in Australia. Bill made up a story of kids going out and skinning the frogs and sucking out the chemicals. James served us one of his wonderfully simple meals of vegetables and steak. Bill drank and smoked poking around at his excellent plate as a kid would, not eating much. After we had finished, James brought out a big bowl of gum drops. Bill grabbed a handful and crammed them in his mouth with some falling into his plate. It was night and Bill heard a noise out back. He had been feeding a critter and determined it was a raccoon by its eating habits. He got a flashlight and took Billy out to search for it. Later James said that it was a memorable evening and it was certainly a great evening for an eight-year old.

Another time, Pam, Billy and I stopped for James' dinner at the Burroughs' cottage. James fixed steak, a favorite of Pam's. "How old's the boy?" He asked Pam, in a typical Midwestern idiom. Billy was eleven then. Bill rolled a joint and poured the Vodka. He was just getting into painting. He brought out some paintings and told us to select one each. He said "this is great art, Charley. Look at them, different things happen in them." Unfortunately, I had to sell them later to pay for the trip. He then got out his blow dart gun, put a dart in it and put it to his mouth. I told Billy to stand in back of us. Bill aimed at the front door and blew the dart in it. "Lucky someone wasn't coming in", Billy said to me aside. Bill tried to get it out of the door but couldn't budge it. He got a pair of pliers and pulled it out. . But I did bring the paintings back to Cherry Valley and put them outside and different shapes did form in them. He then brought out a montage he had made and sat me and Billy down to watch as he, like an old carny, moved about to change shapes. Pam mentioned she would like to do another small book and have S. Clay Wilson illustrate it. She had done Cobblestone Gardens, one which I sent Bill a bunch of old photos to select from for the text. He rummaged around in his bedroom and got a bunch of typed pages. "Here's some I'm working on. Let me know if you need more." He said S. Clay would be a good choice for the illustrations. We called itTornado Alley.

It was in November 1996, Ralph Ackerman and I arrived by train, after spending until daybreak while the railcars humped around in Kansas City. Lawrence predawn. Crossing the East/West border at the Missouri River. Ralph was taking me to San Francisco for an event, the trip a part of it. We got a motel. Pat O'Connor and Rayl met on Mass Ave. in Lawrence. Just like the old days when we arrived on time, whenever that was, with all our equipment, whatever that was. Burroughs had his show up. After the auditorium was the reception packed with high culture. Ginsberg and Burroughs were signing autographs. They got a chair for me in the middle, and I started signing with them. There were so many lines it was as if the signing was the event, and it didn't matter who I was, I was sitting between them, so my signature must be worth something. James fixed us lamb chops that evening at

Burroughs' cottage. Allen helped James with the dishes. Bill and I sat at the table. He was not smoking his English cigarettes, so I could not bum. He put the catalogue for his show on the table. "Look at that, Charley" he said. "A beautiful production, don't you think?" He showed me the paintings in it, explaining each one. He was quite proud of the book and said it was reasonably priced at $25. I asked him for that one, just to put him on a bit. I'll never forget the look of polite embarrassment, wanting to be generous but won't be conned look. He smiled pleasantly, and said, "not this one." He summoned me to his bedroom and Allen made some comments about his chambers, putting some magic to the evening. Bill took out his stash from his drawer with the 38. He told me to sit at his dresser and roll a joint. Allen went to the supermarket with James to get Allen special foods. Ralph wasn't eating. He had throat cancer. "Dr." Burroughs engaged him in medical talk about his condition. Bill, Allen and I each had undergone heart problems in the recent past. The evening had a ceremonial, soiree ambiance. Bill wasn't drinking or smoking. After dinner, James wrote a poem and was encouraged to read it. Afterwards, he handed it to Allen, who began editing it. James was complimentary for having the honor. Allen, who was a professor at City College said humbly, "That's my job." The conversation turned, at my direction to the questions for the panel raised by members of the audience at the lecture, earlier. Those members on the panel were asked what their all-time favorite lines were. Bill quoted "Tomorrow, tomorrow tomorrow", and Allen quoted the couplet from Shakespeare's sonnet "in black ink, my love may still shine bright." I mentioned that they both quoted Shakespeare and Allen wasn't sure from which sonnet. I recited the whole sonnet and told him it was easier to begin at the beginning with it. Allen was surprised I could recite the whole sonnet. Bill peevishly tried to interrupt me about midway through and James gently put his hand on his shoulder.

Ginsberg read my "heart attack" poem to Bill, James, and Ralph Ackerman, remarking about some lines reminding him of Shakespeare. Bill absorbed them, as he seemed to do with words: with larger language components, he seemed ready to cut them up and reassemble them his mind, in cartridges ready to fire. Allen then made some minor editorial marks on the poem.

Bill went to his bedroom and put on his pajamas and prowled deliberately around the house, feeling his canes. He picked up his Mexican-carved sugar skull and talk about it, handing it around. During dinner, Allen talked ostensibly about health and particularly about his diet. He could not eat sugar. I said to Bill, "Well at least Allen won't eat your skull." Bill chuckled and answered. "No, Ginsberg won't eat my skull."

James and I went outside the house to look at the Kansas sky and admire the big cottonwood tree in the yard. Bill came out on the porch clearly restless as in minutes to go. He had been "out there" so he seemed to like being at home with friends, prowling, like one of his cats. His living space always had an awesome feeling. That was the last time Allen saw Bill.

Easter 1997 we met S. Clay in N.Y.C., got blasted and planned to visit Allen. About 11:00 we decide it was too late in the evening to call: we didn't know it at the time, but Allen lay dying. We came to Cherry Valley for a few days. Wilson bought me an Easter chocolate wrench at Dean and Deluca's. Pam got all the sandwich makings and we scored some Elephant beer. Pam fixed a great meal for S. Clay, but he had run down to the Quickway and ordered a large sub. He ate that for an appetizer and then finished his meal, then grabbed Pam's father's sword and played pirate. We drank, smoked and ate for the next few days, bringing the rest of the food from D&D's to Claude and Mary, who lived about an hour away.

In the spring of '97, I drove from Cherry Valley to Missoula, Montana to pick up my son after his freshman year at the University of Montana. On the way back, we stayed with Patricia Elliott, a grand gatherer of fine people. Her family was in the wrecking and salvage business in Lawrence, and she provided Bill with the right doors to shoot. She called Bill as we were leaving and he said to come on by. He had been chatting with one of his friends, a sculptor, a soldier of fortune-looking guy also into guns and knives, etc. who had some mutilated hand guns with him, one that had been run over by tanks in an urban gun program of some sort. He was going to weld one to his metal sculpture and wanted Bill to shoot some high ballistics through it the next day. He handed the guns around. Bill looked at them, and slightly indignant, aware of the old teachings of his class...to take care of things...said, "I don't know why they'd want to do this to a perfectly nice Colt."

After his friend left, he talked to Billy about college. Billy told him that he was dropping out for a while. He didn't want to have the debt. Bill totally ridiculed the astronomical costs for college. And for what? He had a litany of what was taught and who taught the courses. He agreed with Billy that the costs were too high for average young white males. Bill looked melancholically out the window toward Montana, long ago. "My father used to take me fly fishing in Missoula" he said. Later I told Billy he should have asked him some questions. I asked Bill to sign a copy of Western Lands for Billy. Pointing to me he said "...And I have something for you, too." "Oh," I said. "What does it look like. Maybe I can help you find it." It comes in a bottle. He searched around the living room and his bedroom. I followed him around. He seemed remarkably nice; having lost my stash, I would have been aggravated. He said it was a bottle of Codeine. He had signed a book to me "Codeine Charley, all the best Rx." He couldn't find the bottle, so he took me to his medicine cabinet. "Can you take Methadone?" he asked. I said "Yes." He had two small capfuls. "I don't know what your system can take, but drink what you want." I told him that Huncke had once sent me some in an old perfume bottle, complete with Dr. Huncke's instructions and warnings. I finished the one and downed most of the other capful. I told him maybe I should finish it off, that I had a bug I caught in Missoula. He said he wasn't worried about drinking after me. I left a small amount in the cap.

I told him we should push on to St Louie before getting a motel that night. He said. "That will kick in about the other side of Kansas City. Billy got behind the wheel as we waved goodbye. "Via con Dios," Bill waved with his arm making a generous curve over his head. "What a great old man," we said. I crawled in the back of the car and went to sleep. "A Johnson to the last," I thought. A Johnson to the last. I remembered Kansas in the '50...the ethos of the hobohemian hipster, often maligned--to share your shit.

POST-BEAT DINNER POSTSCRIPT

Grant Hart and Laki Vazakas were going to the Patti Smith show at the Bowery Ballroom in N Y C and called Pam and me. Earlier, they had been in Cherry Valley cruising in my 66 Mercury Monterey hardtop convertible (all 18 ° feet of it) and filming with Jamie at a "little speakeasy French Provencal gourmet house" in a valley over the hill from Ginsberg's old retreat. Pam's mother, Mary Beach and Claude Pélieu were celebrating the opening of their show in Paris from which Grant selected a collage for his new CD. I pressed the Merc in passing gear and went around the others in their selections of new foreign cars. Claude gave them all the finger and was ecstatic all during brunch exclaiming he'd been waiting all his life to give those little Jap cars the finger from a "beeg" American car. As we all drove away from the brunch, instead of waving, we all gave each other the finger.

Grant called from the city and asked Pam and me to the Patti Smith concert at the Bowery Ballroom, a sold out-four floors crammed-body to body-with everyone you wanted to be with-show. Patti was more NYC than the Statue of Liberty in torn levis with her fans crowding the stage mouthing her lyrics. She called up the Spirits—the Beats, Punks and Gen X's of Edge Street and sang her poetry in tongues. The energy zapped through the windows to the crowds at the sold out doors...to the jammed intersection where I scanned our once

Bowery loft of the 60's. Even with the V.I.P. tags that Grant had scored, we were just able to see her from the small balcony. I was barely able to maintain life, sucking the air wafting from the Chanel-numbered-five vaginal incense of a wealthy coifed Sephardic princess sitting in front of me. On the balcony across the ballroom were Patti's mother and family to whom she dedicated some songs. Between numbers Patti Smith had the guts of Ginsberg and spoke out about our closing millennium's maladies of reckoning, mentioning the Columbine massacre and the legalization of pot. She called Grant on stage for her encore performance of "Rock-N-Roll Nigger"...Jackson Pollack was a Nigger, Jesus Christ and Grandma Too." (Pollack also came from the great white trash pile that changed the landscape of art forever; he emerged with quantum physics before it too was mainstreamed and Postmodernism a career.) The number was a blowout piece and the musicians let go. (This had special epiphany to me since about a week earlier I attended a reading at a nearby failed state university at Oneonta, NY where I had retired as a tutor rather than keep telling the bewildered young the truth. Ferlinghetti read his numbered poems there to a glazed new-moralityspeak politically corrected marked audience and told the student organizer he didn't want to be mentioned as a beat, but rather as Dr. Ferlinghetti. He didn't use the venue to speak to the youth and the professedly tenured about any undercurrent of truth. Later at a party, Grant sniffed at Ferlinghetti's and an English professor's asses much to their astonishment, and said, well that's the way dogs get to know each other!)

After the Patti Smith show, through the guidance of Jamie, we were able to find a first-class restaurant and ate a late meal somewhere in the East Village behind a shabby metal door marked "First." We found a large booth and gathered chairs for Grant, Jamie and his writing partner, Jack, who had just finished a script about Patti Smith's friendship with the young Robert Maplethorpe, Laki, his friend, Pam, my wife Pam, and Patti's vibrant teenage son, Jackson, who was with Patti's housesitter. Some of the dishes were pasta, duck, and seafood. The food was excellent, but halfway through the meal, Grant noticed a wrenching sound that was supposed to be the background music. After several complaints, the waiter graciously lamented it was beyond his control. His manners and explanation satisfied us that it was the owner's call.

1998 NOTES ON FOUND LSD JOURNALS

The term "Acid" had not been coined when I took two varieties of LSD ---one in a vial from Sandoz Laboratories, and one made by Owsley, sprayed on a blue-grey pill. I went through the experience a half dozen or so times in the early sixties.

I had taken Peyote in the 50's and was a spiritually well-grounded person. During the early 60's, in San Francisco, when I first took LSD, I had also procured pure Mescaline from a laboratory in England, and of course smoked lots of pot...My friends and I ordered LSD for experimental use, and since it was not illegal, a fairly convincing letter and/or letter-head or logo would do the trick.

I read or heard somewhere that every seven years, the cells renew: at least the body cells, so I thought I'd let that happen. I had always been a creative, philosophical person, and viewed the world empirically. I would probably have been considered "at risk," nowadays, another term not connoted at that time. So I was well-suited for "mind expansion."

Anyway, I never took anymore of those kinds of drugs, except recently some "schrooms" in "smoke," which produced at most, a pleasant lethargy. So the question always is: Do I think "acid" is stronger now? Even anecdotal evidence cannot answer that; there are too many variables: The quality of the chemistry, the age of the person, the psychology of the person, the number of "trips," the general progression or re-regression of the racial consciousness, and so on.

I can only offer an opinion, a hunch, that the chemical was much stronger, that the trips were deeper, perhaps more pioneering than of those today. It was an experience taken seriously then, with third eye terror or humor, the utter madness of it seems softened today in New Age cliche, or maybe the human consciousness expands, naturally, anyway, absorbing the fantastic, unnoticed.

One thing I can't understand, is the social imperative to confuse chemistry with morality. It's not the chemical, it's the person. It is fear and irrationality that obsess those who try to eradicate these chemicals; probably the same fear that makes them seek sheltered orthodoxies, or to kill. On L.S.D. in my time, these very flaws and ironies of the human race were prominently part of the lesson. And even then, the expression of these trips were illustriously religious. Gradually, the icons gave way to algebraic fractals and minimalisms, though always suggesting something just over the ridge.

I am left with some general opinions about these classes of chemicals. I have a kinship to the works of those who've successfully used chemicals in their creative assaults into futurism and symbolisms. It would be interesting to know the difference that these experiences made on my life---or maybe it wouldn't. I pretty much take everything for granted, including no answers. Most people still push belief systems, and are suspicious of those who don't do the same. I just tell them I believe in "Belief." To me, there's never much difference between Oz and 'dem.

While digging through my box of old materials, I found a letter to my sister which contained a typed journal. The letter to her was postmarked San Francisco, 1962:

JOURNALS FROM LYSIDIA, 1962

The shucks destroyed; the ripe corn scattered.
Face up. Sly men have no defense.
"For to him that is joined to all the living there is hope."

Rebirth
At Lysidia, the doors fling open and you are there where you always knew you would be. It is the fear you were afraid it was. It is you w/out the Race, the extreme you, the personal you. It is the Race w/out you. You begin to taste yourself. The beast in your face tightens. It is the facts. There MAY or MAY NOT be sympathy from a greater force. It may not tend your ego for it owes you nothing. You can change places with anything in the universe. You are cut away from the years that formed you. You giggle and cry in the flash of mystery. You are intense with bright new meaning. You are Alice in Wonderland. Exaltation is slow and painful. Orgasms are objective energies. Sexuality is abysmal and is performed by your total body. The melting is automatic, there is not seduction or evil gain at another's expense. You may live in another hand or vein.

Impact
No time. All memory at once. No ground wires or name-association. Fear of infinity. Cling to something. (Function of the Orgasm. Creation. Cause.) Absurdity and profundity are the

same but you are over the hump of them both. Everything is on every level. There is no way to tell if anything or anyone is valid. Cling and wait. No one leaves Lysidia. You may hear the weeping laughter of newcomers or see the noise of energy. The language spoken is fragments from a written race or bits of what you tried to say from voices that you used to hear. This does not do the job. Words curl into their own spheres but there is always a communication that keeps you TOO MUCH IN TOUCH. There is a word that not one knows yet it is the word everyone tries to say. You have no identity in Lysidia. You have no time. (Death. Emergence of a New Order of Consciousness.) The cats in Lysidia sleep, like always. Restless, relaxed, yet half awake...as if they are trying to settle something in their sleep. There is confusion or high speed truth, since by HABIT you had formerly termed chaos anything you had not confined.

The Trails
Don't let the grown-ups in; we have to get down to business. Blow flies on a ridge, sun down to your neck. Fear of melting, fear of loving. Spirits struggling up a hill, who will stop them, no one will, till the diamonds of your heart spill, O moonlit man. The surge and flow of the brain. The waterways of Lysidia where tots grow cities in despair. I have brought these journals back. To where? O joyful surge, then back again, round and round the painful bend. Breakthrough, WHO ARE YOU? Internal shudder. Quick messages that sing like superchords and sashes of the sight. The charity of dog and flower. The tissue of birth beating in a friend. Infinite nostalgia. Maybe no one really knows. Who can touch anyone without crying. Pray for those who sleep, may their skin contain their sleep. And if I wake before I die, I praise the Lord my soul to try. Blessed were the days of sunsets, Blessed was the first May wine. Blessed were the young who worshiped and who created. Blessed was their time. Blessed were their exaltations, Blessed were their melting loins. For they were fools, but dear ones. The spider crawling out his silk. The stomach sticky. The moments gone. The body decays into the ground, the

beast kneads daily the face it found. Their efforts confined to beasts who feed upon them because they do not want to know what they do. Meanwhile Moses is the only one who has looked into the face of God.

Little City
And into the panoramic Shortcuts of Lysidia, the face of the Race surged and converged; death, youth, decay, emerged; angels, devils, murderers coated the face with transverse history into a thin translucent burst that ghosted a bio-electronic cling of orgastic destiny. Once more a red hot meal, cloudbursts of gravity that rain ozones and long grapes when sets of waves cancel out each other by arriving at the same time and the lyrics of the ocean is your breath and the interference of light breaks things two by two and onto three with the rhythm of the breath and the rhythm of the wind and the rhythm of sex and song and dances and the rhythm of speech; the rhythm of Botticelli's figures, the rhythm booming Berlioz's Requiem, the purr of a cat, the melting of molecules, the throb of a prick, the caress of a hand, the turn of the century, the change of energy, the madness of the heart, the vanity of the sun, the suck of God, the time and chance of all.

Wings of Matter
Memoirs. "When beauty lived and dies as flowers do now." Then came my cyclonic friends from the plains burnished bare from vortex and 3.2 beer, and saw again Alan, the lion of the lily, whose beauty pours into some vast container which slowly bursts and kills him. And saw the new breed of generals who never pull on their boots, and we took them to Lysidia, Lysidia, the little city of the skull and then disintegrated down the streets of San Francisco that took us where we lived.

Nostalgia
And I lay down on the beach, complacently cosmic, waited on the waves, seasons, and weightless birds. I recalled how I felt as a small boy, when in a private corner I cut my heart with the

toys of a big world. In the green paths of virginal wheat, time was plentiful and the world was everywhere. I ran where I thought I was going while the sun was a solemn caravan crawling over the desert, and the rainbow was candied silence the children ran to eat. I put a cowboy stage atop my head. Through the classroom windows a playground peal beat out the bicycle days. How mysterious the straight obsidian school-marms. How I would have liked to have been pampered and protected by their authoritative bodies--while I learned their secrets. I threw rocks and talked of fortunes. I couldn't stand conventional gears, I spoke of fluid drives and was expelled. And a delicate girl took my by the hand and led me to a mound. At a nearby refinery, gas flames lashed eternally from a pipe in the air, the flame forever in our brows, and to always follow the burning tiger whether he ranged bright or dim to open freedoms' doors of love or hate and all that is beyond them. And I returned to the waves receding and becoming and knew that all this was apart from me, yet, somewhere in separate years, or in Time's latticed mind. I thought life isn't too short or too long, for who can know if there is really enough time in the slow sledge of settling Eternity.

CURLED IN CHARACTER
R. CRUMB AND THE FIRST ZAP

My favorite reality chamber in the 40's and 50's was to cradle myself in the big overstuffed armchair with a stack of comics on the floor and some beside me in the chair a smorgasbord of preferences that would satisfy a reading orgy should I decide to shift quickly from Mary Jane and Sniffles, the first "Lucy in the sky with diamonds" (or dust she sniffed), to Prune Face, The Submariner, Scarecrow--or the old standbys--Captain Marvel, Batman and his Robin, et. al. I might have just traded for some more esoteric ones, "The Thing," a Luftwaffe pilot who went down in the swamp and turned into a swamp monster trying always to resolve his identity, Or "He-She," who turned sideways to foil the police with its sex. One side was a man, one a woman; the first hermaphrodite androgynous transvestite character, who, I'm sure could enjoy great popularity now.

The classics would be shuffled to the bottom of the pile. I would put my classic education off as long as possible; however, they were still better to get into than reading the stilted, pretentious English of James Fenimore Cooper. Oh yeah, and there were ones I could never get the plot, like Little Orphan Annie and Prince Valiant--they were also towards the bottom of the stack. I'd read Bugs Bunny first, or other Disney characters. It wasn't until much later in my scholarly pursuits that I found a couple of references to the metaphysical aspect of

Disney by none other than Ezra Pound, who thought Disney was one of the greatest metaphysicians of the 20th century, who brought us a personified natural world...pretty heavy stuff indeed!

The smell of colored ink and newsprint was an aroma that lured me into the page. As important to me as the stories, were the characters, who were not remote, and certain frames I had to go back to and curl up with a while, dwell on, until I absorbed the full action and context. In this aesthetic, the comics seemed more like movies to me than textual stories. I would imagine getting the characters into a story line would be the most difficult aspect of cartooning. Our linear-literary consciousness culture always wants "the story". There is something also about cartoons that to me had an affinity to old radio shows, which may be just a generational personal feeling rather than an aesthetic, implicit in the art form. Sometimes I would trade for a little fat book made to flip the pages and make the characters move, which is the basis of filmed cartoons. I have regrettably not yet seen any of Crumb's film work by or about him.

Among other delights it was the creation of characters that grabbed me into Crumb's work. Theorizing, in hindsight, those I selected to keep on the top of the pile would have the necessary values that belong to the art; be profane, carnival, or vulgar in the artistic sense. Crumb filled those criteria. His good invention of character, most often himself, and the marvelous idiolects that were not afraid of controversial dialog also set a fearless tone that could go back in traditional literature to Chaucer. He was in the generation of cartoonists with a message, and his characters brought a larger "character" to the form, a whiff of genius compared to the piddling, politico-socio-culture engineering that steers our categories today: feminist, multicultural, new age, and all that which sadly seems to complicate our national character in lies, convolution, complexity and more control. Ironically, most older comics were pretty one-dimensional, or highly skilled in converting any message into acceptable story lines. Obviously Dick Tracy was not a Dick for nothing and was no doubt one of J. Edgar's favorites, tucked in among his confiscated erotic reading material. Comics like American heroes had the simplest story lines though others like Batman and Robin, simple in their ethos, good over bad, had a particular subliminal psychological undertone that has something to do with their lasting popularity.

Crumb is also literary, evidenced in all his work, even in his secondary scholarly creations like his masterful work on Kafka. He certainly should be taken seriously as one of the masters in all cartoon history, not just "underground", (if that designation has not outlived its usage). I remember two comics I bought in a trunk in Kansas at an auction in town ready to be cleared for a lake and dam, incidentally, where Bill Burroughs later went fishing. One was The Katzenjammer Kids, and the other was Andy Gump. They had cardboard covers and the format was almost square, printed on newsprint, with introductions written by famous people such as Mayor LaGuardia and Enrico Caruso.

There has always been a sustained audience for comics, and there is a surprisingly large audience for "underground comics", which I'll talk about later, but the quality of consciousness in underground comix contains a certain realism that still has to be disguised in the mainstream. Think how many high school kids would stay in school if they had these cartoons for their curricula, instead of the most boring sanctified official-governmental socio-soft-Fascism that cleverly and constantly engineers our kids to become economic and cultural slaves to their empires. I haven't followed the New York mainstream press stories and the recent controversy over Crumb's work, but I'm sure it exemplifies what I'm talking about. As our society swells, it divides, and that division is engineered into the mainstream from diversity. In the "doublethinktank," these actions have the counter-effect of creating more identification and control. The boomers and their babes have to have these markers to know the good guys from the bad guys; freedom of speech is too simple for them (or too complex).

One could stand back and watch it happen from a distance; certainly other countries have a different perspective of this country, but I'm still foolish enough to hope that all the cartoonists and their audiences will continue to enjoy freedom, liberty, justice, sex and deprivation--as is tradition. But as we see in today's politics, depicting these historical themes is interpreted as causing the vulgarity it displays. There's no tolerance for exaggerating fat asses in our society, so if the Organization of Fat Asses can make the government engineer them into a nondiscriminatory categorical squeeze in the control box, everything will be right. Oh Yeah.

I think the first strip of Crumb's I saw was in an underground newspaper from the upper Midwest. There were some poets from Cleveland associated with the poet, d. a. levy, who had come to the San Francisco scene during the early to mid Haight-Ashbury and who had given me a paper. I had a larger press in the Mission District at the time. I liked the posters in the head shops that were thriving in the Haight. I didn't care for the religious and flower-power drawings in the Oracle, so I put out a couple of issues of a newspaper I called The Last Times in which I lifted Crumb's strip from the Midwest underground paper. There was a need for more newspapers that the street kids could hawk, so someone was there buying all I could print, which was only a paltry 500 or so copies. I never made any money on them. There is only one person I know who has copies of the papers. I assumed most of them were tossed. I thought they were more exciting than the Oracle, but what did I know? Anyway, poster art was going to dominate the paper scene for a while.

I was into the literary and later the music scene at the time Crumb came to San Francisco, and I had kept an old prewar Multilith and offset camera from the Mission shop. We were having nude parties at the Post Street address from the Gough Street scene which had dissolved. We had complimentary tickets to the Janis Joplin and Big Brother concert, but we were too stoned to get there, though it was only a few blocks. Lots of people dropped by, someone talked about a new group he was involved with called "Pink Floyd". Billy Jharmark of the Batman Gallery, who later gave me his 52 MGTD Classic, and his friend, Bob Branaman who was living in the backseat of his '50 Chevy were still on the scene. Even Huncke visited us at that pad, and we associated him with the disappearance of an IBM Selectric, bless his heart. There was junk on the street and pot in the cupboard.

Bob Branaman was a "finder"; he eventually turned up everyone who was anyone. It was a business deal, or as close as one could come to it that brought Don Donahue to the door. It was supposed to be 5,000 copies, but that's a stretch. I'll tell you why. But first--I loved the drawings Don laid out on the desk. I felt like I was curled up again in that chair and knew that these drawings were important artworks, so I wanted to be identified as the printer, and thus put my name on the bottom of the back cover.

It is amazing how much the printing technologies have change just from the Sixties, and of course, we had prewar equipment, that wasn't really capable of a printing job like Zap Comix. I would have to make the Multilith dance and sing; I took on the job. After all, I was arrested for forgery and uttering when I knew Branaman in the Wichita County Jail. But it was the lack of technology which caused most of the waste in run of what was supposed to have been 5,000 copies...my guess is around 1,500 copies. My wife, Pam says less. I don't think my printer's scruples would allow too much of a rip-off, but most everyone was on acid or pot and was so excited to see the finished copy, and since there was little money and barter involved, I don't know who counted.

Prior to that meeting, I attended a party at Don Allen's, the West Coast editor for Grove. I was trying to get both him and Ferlinghetti to publish Crumb and was also working toward getting Keep on Trucking drawing off Crumb. The literary publishers seemed uninterested at the time, even though I was later paid well ($300 plus) a piece for a couple of poems that were illustrated in Evergreen Review by artists I never knew; I tried to introduce publishers to Crumb, but they had other interests (or tastes).

I explained to Don Donahue that I really needed a chain delivery on the press, which only had a small chute for 500 sheets, and a spray attachment to powder the paper so the colors wouldn't offset on the next sheet. We pulled out small stacks from the chute as I squirted each of the sheets with powder from a turkey baster. The chain-delivery, incidentally was invented by a printer in San Francisco as a Rube Goldberg devise to grip the sheets of paper and stack them in a receding pile (funny how the Multilith Company didn't think of it). Anyway, the chute delivery had two little chrome wheels that ran along the edge of coated cover stock (which in itself was stressing the press's capability). And the images, which by now I had gone over with Don, sending him back to Crumb to make separate color overlays (continuous tone was out of the question), maxed out the 10x15 format of the press. In other words, there was no margin for the wheels to carry, that didn't contain an image. I solved that problem by soaking cotton pads in the water solution and attaching them to the wheels' fixtures with a rubber band.

Mind you, all the sheets of cover stock had to be run through the press four times, for each color, including the black. And registration had to be perfect, so I ran some trial pages with black only, first as a template for all the other colors because I wanted to put on the black ink last, to cover any gap in the registration. In addition, the Multi had to be fine-tuned constantly to hold its register. Even at that, every 10 or so copies the lines would jump out of register a little. This was characteristic for most all machines at the time. I also had to compensate for slight differences in the stock trim, because Don bought it at surplus odd lot paper dealer, and it may have been cut cross-grained or absorbed humidity before the next run. The technical problems were endless. The format remained the same for many years in the comix trade, but it was in a sense arbitrary, because it was the maximum size for a Multilith 1250.

I liked the newsprint, because it was like the old 1917, 1920 editions I mentioned earlier. I forget whose idea it was, probably mine to put the inside on cheap newsprint, which had been used also in some very fine little press poetry books I had from France. But the newsprint was no picnic to run, either, usually newsprint was made for a web press that took it in rolls. It didn't cut out and run as well as #20 bond or book stock. Anyway we completed the job and went to Crumb's apt. for a party. We got high and drank and ate cake. I especially remember his overstuffed armchairs and his old Philco radios. Anyway, the collector's item, "printed by Charles Plymell" is well worth its price; I'm pretty sure the original count was short. The last time I saw one was one I had given a friend's kid who lived on the Bowery. He used to take it down to the Bat Cave in the city and watch its value climb.

It was with some gallows humor that I traded the press to Don, and told him that he could learn printing as well. The darkness compounded when I saw the chaotic struggle of old wiring and mattresses and paper all over the place in his ghetto warehouse. I told him he could expect some waste. Don fought it to its end in Great Balls of Fire. It took courage for me to enter the premises, and knowing all the complications that vex an experienced printer, I looked with sympathy at that chaotic scene, but he excelled in chaos. It served him well. A true Man of the Comix.

It was many years later, while living in Cherry Valley that S. Clay sent word of a Comix show in the city. I hadn't seen Crumb since the first Zap, nor S. Clay, since I printed his first folio on Grist's press when I was working at the Campbell's Pork & Bean factory in Lawrence, KS. The plan to go to this show began the strange comixesque episode in Cherry Valley with a local character straight out of a 60's cartoon, a 70's comic fan, mechanic, dreamer, "Dangerous Dan" his friend, Ray, Mike, myself and Melodie. Ray had an old four-door Caddy with a Bat signal painted on the back. (He went in for a revival fad at the time.)

The line at the gallery was several blocks long. I caught a glimpse of Spain who got us in, but it was packed so much I couldn't get to S. Clay. Crumb came out and was talking to Ginsberg. I tried for a photo but the camera lens was all wet from sweat and humidity in the gallery. I gave it to Melodie who tried to get some shots. I groveled my way through to Crumb to say hello and talked to Ginsberg for a while. People started asking me for my autograph and took pictures I've never seen. Ginsberg turned to me and gestured to the packed gallery and said "See what you started."

The rest of the evening was spent trying to press in to see S. Clay, but we had to leave. On the way home we were stopped by New Jersey troopers who demanded Ray, in his baseball cap get out of the car; he handed them a temporary license, which made the trooper say "What's this, your kinder-garten report card?' One by one we filed out of the car while they searched the trunk. They were sure they had some-thing...but WHAT? Finally, I, an old white bearded man wear-ing a handkerchief around my head, got out and told the troopers that I was from a small village which didn't have many resources and Ray was the only Limo driver I could find. They sensed the paper work would be too much on this scene, so they just told us to keep on going...out of New Jersey. There was a lot more to that cartoon, but it will have to wait. It does seem though, that reality takes on a special nearness when it is near a comic event. In science, It would be called a cosmic event.

I hear that Crumb got some heat from the multicultural fems about ladies with the big butts and the likes. He has cho-sen to live in France. I think that's a good idea. The best way to really see this country crumble, if it isn't in a cartoon, may be from far away.

THE AGE OF RESONANCE
For Paul Bley, New Year's Eve, 1994

The "Resonant Generation," or "Resonance Generation" are the names I will use to characterize the Age of Apostasy. The noun form sounds like, and may undoubtedly be confused with, the "Renaissance," which, in its variant spellings, surely incorporated the resonant attire. Indeed, recently there has been a resurgence of the "Renaissance Man," in an attempt to typify and mainstream our post-modern person, who cannot afford to be narrowly specialized. The revival of that term has an economic ring, or should I say, opportunistic ring to it as in expanding one's portfolio to include more risk. The notebooks of Da Vinci illustrate the point, both in creation and at the auction.

But to reuse an old term to revitalize fashion underlies the definitive need for a more contemporary designation. What would we do with Buckminister Fuller's notebook, Jackson Pollock's, Steven Hawkins', and so on? To use the adjective, "resonant" might be simpler. The Resonant Generation is descriptive enough. Its frequency excitation would surely include the vibrations of recent movements of the past, when the mind was altered or expanded, as well as include the many interrelated alternatives redistributed throughout our post-modern, technical, artistic cross-section maximum volume mix of today and future creative endeavors.

Though the Resonant Generation typifies the last decade of this millennium and represents a force well beyond 2000, its boundaries, like all movements, have edges invisibly feathered in its beginning and end. One could go back to the atomist, Hericlitus, to restate the charm of modern physics (all things are flowing). Or with that probability of the driving frequency equal to the undiluted frequency of the system, one could begin the action with Jackson. (Pollock, that is, of whom one of my colleagues recently insisted that his "control" was entirely intentional and the reason behind his successful masterpieces.) I certainly couldn't have argued the point but amused myself by thinking it would have surely precipitated a binge to regurgitate the exponents by the master.

Or we could begin with Tesla, the mad inventor, whose followers sometimes claim his connection with outer space. He said that "electricity will annihilate space." It has certainly happened through virtual reality. Resonance was certainly the force common to all his inventions and thinking. Or Sheldrake, who advanced used the words "morphic resonance" to account for a commonality of change that happens at the same time, independently, throughout our geographies, our senses obviously impossibly connected; tapping the keys to artificial intelligent is now as natural as learning to crawl, or the sound of a John Cage composition, a noise that arguably could be harmony somewhere in the vast prolongation of sound, though our ears may not atone it. The Mandelbrot equation. How far along its path is the carnival? The spiraling balloon-like image, the grotesque yellows and reds, the overstuffed, the bumpy-gaudy circus patterns we wander in, the clown spirals far out to the edges. But take the equation far enough down in an algebraic corridor and we will enter a Mondrian, a well ordered formation, a neighborhood mode we've known a lifetime, easy to correspond in the colors of the avenues and cross streets.

This is a time when all things are in a flux. Chaos is popular. Language encodes in more than two levels at once. Buffoons rule nations, altruisms and morality are unstable and can be benignly realigned with control and power. Equalities are no longer bound by structures we once took for granted; elasticities of the systems we defensively tried to bond have gone flat. We are dislocated, waving for help out of a destiny that was ordered for us to be comfortable in our lifetime of postwar modern reality. Without change, the resounding cry was too long. The decay of this lifetime was too complex, too subtle to notice. We falsified ourselves to survive it, waiting for a superior human bond that hasn't happened. We were left drunken, feebly applauding some score or movement that evoked a memory, before trying to be first to the toilet. In a timeless blustering wave for help, we captured what we can at the minimum individual action. No one really wants to see it, or hear it again. Every sensitive person feels a bit squeamish, realizing that we are the sickness, the great parody of "We are the World."

At no greater time have individuals walked with such digitally separate minds. Neighborhoods are as foreign to the mental state as vast geographies. There is no analogue of geography or field. On such a small planet, there is only the neighborhood grid, which serves those who need to control, or controlled, who see the world as that grid to conquer on their All Terrain Chariots. We can sympathize with the Athenian, who lived long enough to see the old Greek song of Democracy triumph and thwart the demigods through lyric poetry, to form and socialize classic theater for the new state, only to see that commerce, the worthless goods, and manufacture of standing armies, gave way to individual freedoms, created busybodies who were no longer inclined to live and let live, argue real issues. Above all, we need our creeping Sparta hot and cold to turn our minds, numb and enslave our bodies: or why would black leather be so popular.

If it's not our Athens, it's our Rome, which repeats its destiny. The flying horse logos at the Mobil Station in the little dying village symbolizes control. The armed legions went out into the hinterlands of the Empire wearing armed vests and helmets. The riot police. Across the street, the disciples with rotting teeth and thrift shop shoes inform the police of any criminal activity, hoping to get in good with the legions.

Someday they can even be in the army. Meanwhile, the liquor, gambling, and contraband go on. The State knows it has to let its citizens have entertainment. It's the video and lotto. The only different item in this 2000 year control image is the oil. The ancient land now named Iraq tried to throw in its card. Our young video lads, mostly Christians now, finally, after thousands of years of integrating the armies, blew those ragged, barefoot, conscripts off the desert. They all got metals and took their cybershots to the mall. The yellow ribbons went up. The preacher asked how many had a loved one in the armed forces. The congregation raised their hands. No one asked who paid for it. The numbers are too great. The complexities have cut to its core. Its great expansion and growth have oozed all over itself, poisoned itself.

And we have nothing but old phrases, cliches, jargon hailed again. We have forgotten that we took something for our own. When the Swede turned the sod, the Sioux picked up the dirt and said "wrong side up." Symbolic of our earth's travail now, subsidized depletion until the aquifer runs dry is but another tiny piece of the inevitable unraveling. We try our New Age, which wants the "Old Wisdom." We ride in our Firebirds from the Catskills to California retreating to retreat from ourselves, meditations, Tantras, The Way, The Wise, The Tai Chi-Chi Shaman, guaranteed in oxymoronic Western advertising "the systematic clear teaching style." Overpopulation is indeed the planet's greatest threat, but an overpopulation of fools is immediately catastrophic.

Yet there is a feeling from some remote force that something will come together when needed, at the right time. Something to catch on to, as the old singer laments on the back porch. Someday is here. As this century changes, we will see changes that we cannot imagine. Something is resonating out there beyond this millennium, this delirium. It is our self that has let a perceived change capture us. Some sought the New Age. Some sought spiritual masters. Some went plum fundamental. Some went mental. Some went far out where there is the delirium carnival millions at one eyes and words. Paradoxically, the self embodies all our evil, but it is only the self that can resonate in tune with the remote force we all hunger for. Those invisible creators have known this all along, that's why they must shake their rattle. The vibration is as old as creation. It is still out there. "Step right up folks,"

SPEW ALLEY
(for Uncle Bill)

Some people just can't take the notion that millions of micro tadpole spitfire germs can swim into quiff and get only one hit on the egg, and that becomes us. That wham alone is enough to make one wonder just how come. The chance is as unfathomable as the lottery, the Big Bang, but these little holers make a person. That alone would be enough to spend a lifetime anguishing, just how the easiest and most natural bit of stuff in the world turns into another body complete with its own mind.

And if we just thought of that little mouse hunt and what came from it, we might as well be taken to a padded cell and try to punch our way out of it like a Turet. But then to develop a language, the next most incomprehensible worthless discovery that can express a body! And then it forms itself in a society, learns to make change at the market and learns to compete against the million of other bodies out there, in order not to appear as random as some lone germ, for a germ without a purpose is just another germ, so a body has to pick and choose its social structure, if it's lucky, or be cast into some lot to task itself out to nether end. The best thing of course, is to invent, discover, be a rock star, make money to occupy one's time.

That would be quite enough for a body not to think about the basic reporters' questions too often as applied to the ultimate abstraction. It is distraction that we must have. Escape, anything to ease the pain of the awareness that swells up and won't go away sometimes, like asking what am I doing here, someday I won't be here, what was this, where will I be and what did I know, etc. It is not considered a real pain of course, like a broken bone, so it has to be considered a mental pain, and drugs that can help it are confused, so the whole reality of it becomes ever more convoluted and ends up like everything in the social body that prevents any attempt at understanding because usually it is not in economic demand. The drift is always to the physical, the tangible, the saleable, which uses up the body in disaster. This portends the future for the larger body as well.

Even if a body's purpose was pretty well programmed and adjusted to the selections (religious, political, social) confines of its time, there is the larger purpose that might seep through those confines and wrinkle the whole thing at any given moment. That is also not considered painful, but a condition of life.

Some think the body, oneself, the person next door, et. al. is a cancer that ultimately destroys its host. In this case, we have the planet earth which is showing signs of regurgitating--just like those bodies who took the time to reflect--prophesied. There are ones who say this is just like all the rest of time and nothing happened before; these are usually the ones comfortable in their own social, religious, economic structures and have taken their fate the same as their nicely-mown lawn which my neighbor is doing now on his little tractor. He is making his own pollution as he goes, his pastime deadening his brain cells as he burns the products of a large cartel. He has a flag that symbolizes his freedom (and the cartels) hanging from his garage. He and his society would not see themselves as a cancer, and their pain is usually relieved by Advil or whatever is advertised on television to keep one of the largest financial cartels in business, serving the needs of the society of lawns.

People don't like to see themselves as a cancer, or a virus, even though if we condense history to repetition of human activity, we come up with the same story, the same actions, usually in the form of religion and politics, to administer an over-purpose, or medication in event the individual purpose goes awry. This isn't classified as pain, because it doesn't have the clinical appearance of eating one away. But there is no cure for it. In the religious worlds, it might be assigned to the devil, but in reality, the devil is just like the Ebola, which erupts all organs in blood and bile through all orifices. In the larger world, with all the ports of entry, such gruesomeness is not seen. And our thinking, our math, our best minds of a generation, gave us the end in a far less gruesome fashion. We don't see it happening in all of industry; while the internal combustion engine adds to the whole demise.

The symptoms are decay, daily, brain deterioration. More and more people wonder, and say there must be a reason for what's happening. Cumulatively, the state of affairs for humans has never before looked quite as grim. And given the fact that we've recorded almost 50,000 wars, and our best minds came up with the weapon to "end all wars," commensurate with the whole premise. Still, poetically, when the latex fills the pod under the hologram of the western sunset, the doctor will have legitimate patients to tend. Sit at show window. It's academic. It is said when lightening strikes that one's hands become clammy, one's hair stands on end, and one has three seconds to lie on the ground in a fetal position; that's enough spark for me.

PROPAGANDA AND WAR: THE MILITARY INDUSTRIAL COMPLEX BECOMES THE LAW ENFORCEMENT/CONTAINMENT INDUSTRY

REEFER MADNESS IN THE AGE OF APOSTASY

The system is eating its children as the synergy of substance abuse and crime becomes the number one problem. Society is in a quagmire because we have been in the wrong war. Sound familiar? When we are sucked into something too deep, too complex, we proceed in ignorance and political expediency; the firepower of our solutions inevitably sinks us further.

This war too is about politics, ideals, morals, but corruption provides the fuel. Prohibition breeds corruption as we have learned in history. It also creates profits that have built nations and governments at the expense of its citizens. Now, while we build more prisons, we release violent murderers and rapists to make room for nonviolent deadheads who use LSD and pot. Under mandatory sentencing, the drug user often does more time than the murderers.

This generation does not have Eisenhower to warn of the "military industrial complex." He was trying to tell us his vision of the future where generations got trapped in a cold war that kept people psychologically unenlightened and defensively overkilled for generations. Implied in his warning was the extent a psychological war had to be escalated in order to keep the industry cranking. He had seen the problems both as a military officer and as government official.

Most judges, lawyers, police, and those who work in the legal system oppose mandatory laws. The mayor of Baltimore, who came out for the legalization of drugs, realized that his best friend, a policeman was shot over a few ounces of costly chemicals. We do not yet have the number of innocents who were killed in the line of fire in drug-related crimes. But it is the politician who wants to keep the issue focused on locking up all the drug offenders. While the inhumane sentencing of harmless drug offenders makes good politics, the big operators go free and violent crime is created, the price of drugs regulated just like our economy. The politicians keep the violent crime drug picture alive because it is easier to run against crime than solve the problem. They believe they represent the morality of Americans, even though these morals have nothing to do with ethics, ideals, or truth.

The propaganda that fueled the cold war became so insidious on both sides that it enlisted innocent people to kill, took casualties up to the last moment, ruined untold lives. Eisenhower had the personal experience of having power over the lives of the Rosenbergs during the time the atomic secrets were known anyway. This possibly formed his belief that there may come a time soon when all of this untold suffering was needless. That time came. All of a sudden the props and the propaganda were no longer needed. Communism was a worthless threat. The enemy no longer existed. There was no reason for a nation to become slaves to producing firepower. The enemy was history. Or was it? What would a nation do now without an enemy, without a war? Look no further. Remember the daily news of Vietnam on television, in the papers, the photos of the helicopters rescuing soldiers from the jungles and the occasional daring journalist's documentation of the good guys razing villages while kids were crying in the background, or perhaps an old woman or man or religious leader wiped out because he was in the line of fire? We have replaced those pictures now in our new war. They are of our living rooms. Not yours and mine, but they could be. All it takes is the wrong informant or the wrong information.

Judges have even wept over the stiff mandatory sentences they have to give to the young. I shared that sorrow when I saw one of many newscasts from Albany about drug busts. The anchor people seem to turn on the dramatics when drug busts come on. They are aware of the high ratings of real shows like "Cops." They have an audience fed on fear. The news story showed a pathetic young man with no shirt or shoes receiving the mandatory five years minimum for 100 pot plants he had been growing all winter in his apartment.

I have spent many years teaching college courses in maximum security prisons like the one he was sent to. Here is a likely scenario: He could easily be raped by a gang, usually weight lifters who wait for young flesh. At first the young inmate would resist, but he would be brutally overpowered; when the fifth or sixth person has entered his ruptured and bleeding anus, he most probably will have resigned himself to being submissive. His emotional and psychological life will have changed. What will he be like when he gets out? He won't be the foolish entrepreneur trying to beat the system of unemployment lines and minimum wage jobs at the franchises, thinking of all the quick pot money he could spend on sports cars and stereos. He is now next door. His neighbors now have a good reason to fear. He now has nothing to lose because he has lost too much already. "On the street armed and dangerous."

The ancient Persian Empire, according to Herodotus, trained the young in truth. No Persian, not even the King, ever punished an inferior for a first offense. Most civilizations were and are civilized about chemicals ingested by individuals. The Persians thought that there was truth in wine, but not the whole truth; for any decision made when they were sober they would reconsider when they were drunk, and any decision made when they were drunk, they would reconsider when they were sober. Herodotus also noted the barbarians who lived beyond the Greek Islands, who smoked hemp rather than drank fine wine.

Substance "abuse" will always be with use. For some, it is the truth. We have stripped the Native Americans not only of their land, but of their religion, by putting drug laws against

the Peyote cactus they have used in their religious cere-
monies. We stopped the possibilities of formal empirical
knowledge about LSD when we made it illegal. There were
casualties, but to what extent, and in what number, compared
to what possible benefits? Why do people still take it, if not to
expand their consciousness? Seeking truth should be an
innate right of the individual even if they do want to pursue
Blake's axiom, "The road of excess leads to the palace of wisdom." Why is it that the Peruvians have always ingested
cocaine, if for nothing else but to work in high altitude? Why
can they take cocaine socially, where here it is combined with
guns and crime? Why can the European youngsters drink
wine if they choose, while here there are serious problems
associated with it? Perhaps we are not civilized. Perhaps we
have been so nurtured on aggressiveness, greed, competi-
tiveness, psychological wars and power, that as a country
dealing with the drug problem, we have become insane.

But we do enjoy seeing the "bad people" on the news
every night getting what's coming to them. Witness the number of programs that specialize in the drama of the Swat
Teams busting down doors, moving according to procedure,
dashing from room to room, cuffing the women and men,
forcing them to spread eagle while the children cry hysterical-
ly. These images will certainly stick in those children's minds
forever.

Just last week the "combat team" got the wrong floor,
the wrong room, and the wrong person. I wonder what the old
Black minister was thinking when he saw those guns drawn,
those masks, those helmets. Brown shirts or blue; brown eyes
or blue? What did he see in his mind as he died looking down
those barrels of semiautomatics. To us it is live drama, film
noire. To him and the children? To the many innocent and
guilty who have provided us this reality staging?

And who are the armed men? Unfortunately, many of
them are the same ones who were in the jungle. They are
highly trained for this kind of work. They get extra points on
their affirmative action applications. To them it's always the
same answer; they are just following orders, just doing their

job...on your kids and mine on our sisters, your brothers, your fathers and your mothers, and it's a lot better than soldier's pay.

Of course some of them take dope, some sell dope. And let me make the pronoun clear. "Them" is all of the above, those who bust down the doors and find the contraband as well as those who use it or sell it. Of course not all those on either side are always guilty. But some are. Those on one side of the door are usually guilty and are usually sent to prison. Some aren't guilty, yet are sent to prison. Some are set up. Some are put in prison for just being high and around dope. On the other side of the door, the uniformed guilty are sometimes sent to prison, but are usually just reprimanded because they are the Enforcement Containment Industry.

Of course, most of them doing the busting do not engage in criminality, but enough do to make the news. Again, just last week there were three narcotics officers in Queens who were busting dealers and dopesters and reselling the stuff. It is not an uncommon occurrence to have those in control take the money and the drugs for their own use. This activity is easily concealed, so we probably see less of it reported than does actually happen. But if we are to be concerned about morality and punishment in this war, we need to be aware. Or beware.

The combatants are once again protecting us by going into the metaphorical jungle, the streets. They belong to the fastest growing industry in the country. It has full support of the politicians with our money. After all, something has to be done with all those who are involved with the highly profitable trade the politicians let slide. Again, the taxpayers in our nation will foot the bill, just as we did during the cold war when we built our military industrial complex, while other nations such as Japan spent money on their own people. Could that be why they have less crime? We have to pay again; the bill for imprisonment of our own may be much higher than shooting the enemy.

Some movements in the war are more obvious than others. In the sixties, when the CIA was experimenting with LSD on unknowing subjects and each other, stories would leak from time to time. LSD was good for mind games and fed a lot of James Bond scripts. The army found that soldiers couldn't march in rank and file and tended to wander off and do their own thing. Of course marching in rank and file could be seen as the greater human aberration; nevertheless, the army gave up its experiments.

By the mid-seventies, what began as mind alterations in the Haight-Ashbury moved toward self realization and established the new age movement of "clean" dopers and "me" health and wealth. Reagan had changed his politics, big business, which used to be his liberal line to big gov'ment, went where the money was, cranked up the military industrial complex, filled unused bases with drug lord goodies, got his friends into the Betty Ford clinic to just say no, and left town leaving us with the tab.

Money, of course, is the real power in our country and has been called our religion. Even with drugs, it seemed that if the lifestyle was associated with wealth, it was morally better. Free enterprise runs deep in our heritage. Roosevelt's family on his mother's side brought Opium from India to China on the fleet of sleek clipper ships. The Kennedy empire had its seeds in prohibition, the secret government used heroin as barter during Vietnam, new skills in smuggling were developed, such as putting the stuff in bodies shipped in body bags.

Wealthier than political parties, the cocaine cartel flourished and deals were made. The news still surfaces about Noriega and the Reagan-Bush associations. The latest one involves the then landing field in Arkansas, where the clandestine air freight business allegedly ran guns to the Contras and cocaine back to the States. No wonder the President is sensitive to the drug issue and forgets quickly his campaign rhetoric about the problem. No wonder President Reagan chose Governor Clinton of Arkansas as one of the nation's best governors. Or is it just the political expediency of offering a few deadheads for a health care program? We'll never know. With mandatory sentencing, we could see deadhead lifers costing the Law Enforcement and Containment Industry $900,000 each. With more prisoners than any other industrial nation, we still want to expand the industry. Here we go again, Mr. Reagan...er Clinton!

The worst thing about pot was that one might end up in a VW bus following the deadhead concerts and not have motivation to make money. The threat of them cluttering the public parks and panhandling or spreading disease was just too risky. Besides, whoever heard of being soft on crime? There's no money in that. I can't imagine writing a grant to travel to schools with a program of tolerance and compassion and smoke pot to show how, like a squirrel, I can't make up my mind what to do. Remember the crazy cockroach? "La cucaracha, porque no fumar marihuana?"

Like the Persians, I would then try to solve the same problems, or do the same tasks, without being under the influence of drugs. It's very simple. Show real danger and effects and gain real knowledge. Most kids figure it out for the best, anyway, without all the stupid drug programs that loom in their schools like a haunting specter of the hunted and the threatening evil, which, in reality, turns out to be none other than our big drug profits-politically sanctioned-propagandized doublespeak of the Enforcement Containment Industry.

In our schools, we finally had to admit that students were given mostly propaganda about the evils of Cannabis. The old notion about going on to something stronger held a while, but empirically, it could hardly be established as necessarily a causal sequence. Sure, if you turn your life over to drugs, you're more than likely going to try them all. But, in most cases, individuals who gravitated to one drug or another were prejudiced against the other. Speed freaks or junkies would have no use for acidheads; old alcoholics might blame potheads for all the evils, etc. There are ancient people around who have smoked weed all their lives and have never used anything else, except perhaps alcohol and cigarettes. Gradually, the medical profession and the governmental pamphlets became more accurate. However, to some, Cannabis, over a long period, could be harmful to the immune system or the lungs. Of course spraying it with paraquat would make it worse than most toxins and pesticides we ingest. Cannabis is not nearly as harmful as nicotine, or the other dangerous toxins put in tobacco.

The most difficult admission the pamphleteers had to make was that marijuana is not addictive. Most anything can become habitual, or most anything taken over long periods will produce side effects. The most harmful chemicals that some ingest or inhale are in everyday spray cans or bottles under the sink. The schools have programs that teach kids to be "stoolies" and even to inform on members of their families. But schools do not have programs that teach how dangerous "huffing" can be, and can share the blame for kids who are afraid of getting caught with pot having huffing parties with legal, dangerous chemicals. There are many young people who are into "huffing" but few educational programs address the practice. Why? They are made by the legal industries, who run our government-by-lobby, and at worst, they would only commit white coat crimes such as tampering with the tobacco.

Still, the sentencing for marijuana can be stiffer than for murder, rape, or robbery. In New York alone 65,000 inmates are doing hard time on drug charges, even though the head of the New York Correctional Association says the laws are ineffective; they've been around for over 20 years and the drug problem has only gotten worse. The Rockefeller laws require life in prison for certain drug transactions, some involving relatively small amounts of illegal substances. Most of us have probably heard of the cases in the Midwest where some young people have been sentenced to life in prison without parole for just being involved with the shipment of drugs.

One woman, a deadhead, writes a letter in "Relix, the classic rock magazine" from a prison in Nashville where she is serving a 92- year sentence, more time than a mass murderer or someone committing a heinous crime. She was with someone who had LSD, though nothing was found on her or in her house. Many deadheads write about their pitiful circumstances from behind bars. One warns of informants for the DEA posing as deadheads at concerts.

As someone who had all the legal LSD I wanted around the house and was on Haight St. before the Head Shop or Jerry Garcia (I saw him impolitely startle a little old Russian lady, perhaps on his first visit to the area,) I cannot imagine the punishment and the way in which deadheads are followed and sometimes set up for using LSD and pot...or expressing their lifestyle. To have informants working in that venue is obscene and evil, and they belong to a "justice" system. What right do we have to chastise other countries about human rights?" We know it is the "just-us" system who selects who it wants to put away, or who should control the dope.

When I taught at Jessup Prison, located between Baltimore and Washington, I learned a lot about sentencing. Recently on television, I saw one of my students being released through a program to let the elderly out. We talked and wrote a lot about crime and drugs. Many of the offenders were doing hard time for nonviolent crimes. Well over half should not have been there, and a certain percent should never be on the outside. But sentencing has little to do with justice or truth, and the "three strikes" proposal will never effect that reality. It will cause more injustice.

Inmates are quick to separate truth from lies, reality from fakery. For instance, one knew that he might be there because he was on Georgia Avenue shooting up heroin in a doorway. He also knew that if he were white, sitting in his Mercedes with MD plates shooting up in Georgetown, he would not be in prison.

Washington D.C. would probably hold the record for more injustices per square mile that any other area. Forget the comical war maneuver from the Drug Czar who had his troops develop technologies of infra red devices from helicopters. This was Dick Tracy come to life. Marijuana plants in California zeroed in on from the air and zapped from helicopters. Women standing outside the post office in a suburb of Washington carrying placards reading, "Help Stamp Out Marijuana." This while the news carried stories about the boom in construction of banks in Miami to hold the cash of the drug trade. This building boom was finally regulated, more from governmental embarrassment than anything else.

In the late 70's and early 80's, my wife worked in the District while I taught in prison. The people with whom she worked were the young professionals who ushered in the eighties. Cowboy boots and hats from Texas and California rancheros replaced the Jimmy Carter pressed jeans of the poor mother's sons and daughters. High powered Volvos with California plates driven by brass hatted or well creased men and women in uniforms, or the uniform of the armies of young Republicans, blue blazer and khakis, zoomed down the avenues crushing squirrels or turtles, or anything else that got in their way. Bumper stickers were already stuck on their new 4x4's, "Neutralize Mondale." The high visibility professionals, the newsmakers, the leaders of industry and politics, the household names were taking over the scene...and the dope.

We were invited to their parties where in adjacent rooms smoke from the pipe and lines of coke were for the taking. I was older, so I discretely avoided the young professional's dilemma of whether or not to invite me into the room, but it was a very common scene at the sociable "chili" parties of the George, Jr. crowd. Anyone who still tries to stereotype drug offenders may be surprised to know that they cross all political party lines and all socioeconomic groups. The New York Times once researched the problem and learned that as a group, the health care profession contained the largest number of substance abusers. I wonder what it might be today? More surprises? Perhaps the law enforcement agencies? We'll never know.

In parts of the District, other than Georgetown or the Mayor's Office, drug busts and violence were a daily routine. The dope was of less quality, probably more potent, PCB, or nowadays, it would be crack cocaine. People who could afford it got the better stuff: the others, bathtub poison. At Johns Hopkins a study was done with marihuana to prove that it didn't affect the inherent moral values of an individual; yet, in Wichita, Kansas huge billboards still decry it as sin.

There was a surge, a money binge that synergized with drugs during those years too. Eventually, it helped produce our great debt. But the greatest debt is probably the quality of life that suffered. When there are not enough opportunities to live decently, there will be more crime, more hurt, more poverty of spirit, more dangerous drugs and more inclination to use them.

I recently took my son to visit Ike's hometown, Abilene. Ike lived across the tracks. Not down so far as Texas St., where in all cowtowns, the cowboys from the trails got rowdy and shot things up. Ike would never be involved with anything like that. His father was a hard-working milk bottler in a dairy barn. My son and I had recently worked for a dairy farm in Upstate, New York, which bottled its own milk, so we could appreciate the history. But make no mistake, those on the "right" side of the tracks looked down on those Eisenhowers from Texas. He chose the right career; he could gain a class unto itself. I wouldn't dislike him for that. In fact, that was the slogan during his political campaigns, "I like Ike." Everybody liked Ike, well, maybe not everybody. Truman thought that Ike was given the presidency for being a war hero, even though he swore to Truman that he'd never be in politics. But he did give us a warning of the military industrial complex, which in Waco, Texas came true.

Times were simpler then. Lots of people say it should be more like the good old days now. I agree. I don't know how old. Back to Coleridge's day, perhaps, when he went to the chemist to get his bottle of Laudanum, then went home to sleep though the cold night, and in an opium vision, wrote one of the greatest poems in the English language. Or how about Poe when he went to the pharmacist to get a little ball of hashish to help him write through the night? Or Lewis Carroll, and on and on? And when our children go on to higher education, they will be indoctrinated into that great discipline of the father of modern psychology, Sigmund Freud, who snorted a "mountain" of very pure coke during his lifelong experiments with many very willing subjects.

Or how about the fellow I'm reading now, who wrote about the annals of U.S. criminals in the late 1800's? He visited an opium den on Mott St. in NYC. He laid out all his belongings and money on a table in another room before he went down the dark hallway into a den where he lay and smoked the pipe. After several hours he went back and got his belongings, which hadn't been touched by the many who came and went. He later came off the influence of opium and got such a headache that he never went back. Yes, those were simple times. Where was the crime in his experience? He didn't even have to worry about his wallet being stolen. Imagine that today.

Or how about Woodstock, where thousands of people tripped on LSD and pot and had no significant trouble or crime (except for the taking of drugs)? Think of all the young people doing hard time now for the same nonviolent act. Think of what would happen if thousands of drunks gathered in a field. Legal alcohol is a problem. Would legal drugs be a problem? Not until we add profit, do guns and violence enter the picture.

There is something indeed wrong with the picture I see on television. Before we explore the picture, I would like to tell my vision of the future. I'm from Kansas too, and my hometown was so small there was nothing but prairie on the other side of the tracks, but I do remember my father inviting the Mexicans who worked on the road gangs to our house to bring their families and play their music. I remember the beautiful and happy music and their children so bright-eyed and happy as their folks sang and played. What I didn't know (well, that was in the 40's; I was born in the dust bowl in 1935) was that it was common for these people to grow marijuana along the railroad tracks to smoke. They, of course, didn't run the trains; their jobs were fairly rhythmical and laborious, tending to the tracks. And they may not have even smoked on the job, but waited until they got home at night to drink the "cervesa" and tequila, which went down smoothly with the marijuana smoke as they sang about the cockroach. The children all seemed healthy too, though I suppose as babies they may have had smoke blown in their faces to put them to sleep or Paregoric or Tequila rubbed on their gums at teething time.

Yes, those were the good old days. Now I would have to turn all of them into the officials if the children weren't trained enough in school to turn in their own families. The Swat Team would have to bust their meager door down, and the children would have to be taken away and given to the state, perhaps an institution where the superiors could frequently abuse them. When were the good old days? Were they in San Francisco, where I could send off for vials of LSD from Sandoz Laboratories? Or send away to British laboratories for bottles of pure Mescaline? Or send to Texas for a box of Peyote buttons? Or go to Golden Gate park where marijuana smoke was so heavy that park policemen had to walk their horses through it?

Though I am no Ike, nor pretend to be, I would like to tell you my vision and then put together all the alarming pieces of what really might be happening to our country. It may be taking a greater toll than our other wars. It certainly has the elements of psychological propaganda. What really does make sense? There have always been inaccuracies in the pamphlets of drugs, and for a while it seemed that drug literature was becoming more accurate. But at the same time the problem itself became more propagandized, more complex, more irrational, and a great deal more power-centered. In fact, compared to the "good old days" the drug war, its czars, its agencies have brought the problem to an alarming level, inexorably tied to the crime problem itself. Now, Clinton has a photo opt with the President of Mexico, while bales of pot burned to show that we can renew loans to Mexico. Meanwhile their methedrine cartel fuels the Midwest.

This is why I, like Ike, feel I have to, as each citizen should, keep track of what is happening. For it seems the problem is purposefully becoming so complex that it will become, or has become, a thing in itself, feeding on its own momentum like a Farm Bureau or other government agency-monsters out of control, spewing out such laws that would purposely confound anyone-mandatory, draconian, growing to such extremes that solutions are impossible. Only the final one, which always preys on the human factor and appeals to the eradication mentality.

"It's the system" has the same meaning as "just doing our jobs." If crime is our number one problem, and we have more than a million people behind bars, why fill the prisons with nonviolent drug offenders? An article in the January 24th issue of The New Yorker states that, "Absurdly harsh sentences mandated for drug cases, and often imposed on nonviolent first offenders, have in many instances forced the early release of violent convicts." Is there a war room that has issued a demand-side reduction to the war and has recommended the following tactics for the Czar: Give the drug offenders stiff sentences (which will please the voters), release the violent criminals (which will cause more crime), build more prisons (which will put people to work), lock up all the offenders who broke the law (which makes the country once again safe). That would please everyone, except the plan falls apart. With more than a million people behind bars and growing, we would soon need half of the nation to guard the other half.

Something could be done immediately about the crime associated with drugs. Make drugs worthless now before it is too late. I foresee that if our nation does continue intact, and its problems, crime being the major one, do not tear it apart, in the 21st century we will look back on the last thirty years or so of this century as the dark ages in our handling of the drug problem. And I predict that we will have to face and solve this problem soon, in this century, because world stability is at stake. The drug problem manifests itself on a global scale as well as on an individual scale. It moves into nations as it moves next door. It is just a matter of time, watch the pictures on television and read the newspapers stories, soon the many pieces may start to cohere, and when they do, you might become as alarmed as I am. The picture has moved to my sleepy rural village. One of the biggest cocaine operations in the U.S. was recently busted nearby. A marijuana farm was raided, the artillery seized. It is common for people here to think like Rip Van Winkle. In their minds, they probably think that it happened very far away, or a long, long time ago. But let a kid in school just act like he has drugs and they go into a frenzy. Stop sending kids to the drugged schools and see how fast the problem is fixed.

I heard about the drug problem in the 50's, I heard about it in the 60's and 70's, I heard about it in the 80's and now the

90's. It is quite reasonable to expect a country, that in my life-time developed the technology to go to the moon and discovered the genetic code (to name a couple of things that would astound all the thinkers of recorded time), would be able to overcome the problems of chemicals that can create criminality that destroys us, at least easily identifiably chemicals. There is probably as much or more harm done to our minds and bodies by the toxic poisons that we purposely emit into the air in the name of progress and civilization.

Gore Vidal concluded in his essay that fighting drugs is as nearly as big a business as selling them, and the American people are as devoted to the idea of sin and its punishment as they are to making money, so the situation will only grow worse.

ANNE AND NEAL AT 1403 GOUGH ST.,
SAN FRANCISCO, 1963

"Work with me Annie,
Let's get it while the getting is good."

........*Hank Ballard and The Midnighters*

I remember Anne, most of the time sad, sometimes sob-
bing, though retaining a strangely fateful, cheerful, glamour of
someone who had been fucked a lot. A West Coast Girl, to be
sure, her dream was an acting career, but she got hooked up
with a guy and lived out a movie slightly unawares fairy-tale,
Marilynesque. Sound familiar? It was the stuff of all drama; a
great, yet seminal drama which many were lucky enough to
touch, watch, play a cameo. I am one of those.

Neal wheeled his '39, (maybe a '40, prewar, anyway, it
had a gearshift on the floor, which would be predominantly
used in syncopation to Neal's stream of
consciousness)...PONTIAC ...into the narrow driveway just
before the sunset of 1963, jerked on the hand brake and was
around to Annie's door while greeting, meeting, and kissing
anyone who was nearby. It was San Francisco, after all, where
spectacle was always the norm. With Gene Kelly's stride and
Popeye's chivalry, he carried Annie across the threshold of
their new pad at 1403 Gough St. I shared the long flat with
them.

Neal spoke with lots of parenthetical asides, redundan-
cies....and emphasized SOME WORDS which became asso-
ciative polymers to kinetic thought and energy. He had a
Hobo's luggage ensemble, a few cardboard boxes containing
underwear and socks, and extra pair of jeans and plain white
T-shirts. Maybe an extra pair of Penny Loafers just to make the
shoeboxes look authentic. He kept them to clean the pot in;
usually smoked in the morning after breakfast (Anne at the
stove, disenchanted, trying to get things right), dinner time,
evenings, (complicating the decision whether or not to walk
over to the Family Dog or whatever the night was about to

unfold), and smoked again into the wee wee hours of the morning. He was paranoid over slight things, just like the benny heads I'd been running with from K.C. to Denver and California, riding over old western trails. His collection of belts caught may eye. They would leave pink welts on Annie's perfectly formed and firmed cheer leader's ass.

The tapes were unreeling to the sidewalk as Neal spoke of his medium in Palo Alto, who had a big body full of water in order to receive the messages of past lives, and so on. He stole something and later told Jesus about it on the way to the cross. The martyr for all pill heads, sneak thieves, transients, pot heads, poor working class unemployed or working and those who are otherwise suspect to the state because they don't accept greed, commerce, and lies as American altruisms.

He laid Annie down on the mattress on the floor and placed his boxes around the room, a grocery sack of black mota weed on the shoe box lid. I had left a stepladder in the long, dark, hallway that ran through the flat with its high ceilings and seven rooms. Neal slid under the ladder, groping himself saying, "just like Playboy magazine, eh Charley?"

Anne resembled Shirley MacClaine, and the Bridie Murphy factor was also there. I suppose there are many people who have more than one personality and that one personality is pretty much straight ahead and could be tiresome in its expression, improved only through intellect, or mind altering drugs. Neal could be defensive in his need to be the story teller and center as he sped up his words and associations.

Having lived most of the time in the Northeast after knowing Neal in San Francisco, I've grown used to art and poetry as a fetish, something those who read the *New Yorker* magazine wait to flaunt after the fad is over; but Californians tend to ignore high culture, live out their contingencies, and Neal responded to that flux by keeping several networks going at once. His chivalrous task was to husband Anne's changes, especially the sexually aroused Lupine one that we saw through the keyhole. Neal, not an ounce of fat on a muscular body, and Anne on top, fucking 'till her knees are sore, nipples hard and erect, and her incisors lengthening. His personality was fairly mainframed. It wasn't long before he ran out of a fuck and slap session telling me to look at her cheeks in which he claimed more Lupine features transblended. Or he would point to her and say, "Look at her incisor growing longer and sharper." She did have "a look for each photo". Her two teeth seemed to get more pointed.

At times Neal would act like it was all too much for him, a hard working stiff, a dumb blonde, a wife, a girlfriend, typically American, paranoid over whose going to rat you out for smoking pot, or being FREE IN AMERICA. Always the other man or woman waiting on his love. He just wanted them all. Underneath it all, Neal was fairly lovable, even in triangles but traditionally had to claim his girlfriend. Anne was lovable too, but the argument took place most all the time, sometimes while fucking or driving; any physical activity syncopated to the eternal argument, in which Anne presented her case, something about never being able to work on her career, always hung up with a married man who won't leave his wife, never mind, his homosexual lovers. The nebulous-affairs arguments that dominate the whole of American song and life. Anne and Neal burned the American Ethos at both ends.

The only break in the nebulous-affairs arguments was when Neal had to browbeat Anne into scoring a script for some speed, or doing whatever she had to do to get amphetamines or pot. Single-minded, strong-willed Aryans tend to like speed. My cabinet was well stocked with laboratory Mescaline and Lysergic Acid, but I don't recall Neal tripping...maybe a little mescaline. Anne, like many a bloomed flower child, liked wine and pot.

Neal would act like a choir boy when they visited Gavin Arthur, the Seer of San Francisco, who would peep on his visitors while jacking off in the kitchen, pretending to fix his drink. They tried to act like normal, new lovers, but soon the restlessness became a conversation of bullet-words. Sometimes they would hold hands, or he would vault over a parking meter while Gene Kelly-ing down Lark St. toward Van Ness Ave.

He got a job at a tire-center, changing tires all day. This was part of "Dr. Ginsberg's" program to rehabilitate this wayward Gentile to do all things normally/simultaneously, like a good husband, wife cheater and beater should, while being a good blow job for Allen.

I would sometimes take him to work on my motorcycle; he always wanted to be in control, so he was a little uncomfortable riding behind me. He had a fretting, worried mind and would tell me to look out for potholes, railroad tracks and every other potential danger. It was not long before he became a star at the tire place. He worked so fast and furiously, the others stood around and watched him. He was always worried about getting to work on time, or Anne's having breakfast ready; he would take out his railroad watch and calculate the exact minutes it would take us to ride to work unless the light changed.

It was early one evening when Allen Ginsberg heard some noises from Neal's room. He motioned me over and peeked through the keyhole. It was the argument with Neal slapping Anne around while he rammed his cock to her like riding a bucking bronk. Then Anne would get on top of him and subdue him and become lupine try to suck the life from him. Upon hearing them slapping and arguing, Allen asked, Is he ACTUALLY hitting her? I said it sounded real. It was pretty hard-core S and M, that's what it was. Both adults consenting.

Anne was primping in the car the next morning, checking her face for the slightest signs of a rough evening. Neal was checking the car's oil and tires. Allen was fumbling with his cymbals and camera. I got in the back seat with Allen. By the time we got over the Golden Gate, they got into it, arguing about what happened the night before, the night they argued. As we were wheeling around the narrow coastal highway, Neal was slapping Anne, downshifting, grabbing the handbrake, and trying to keep the car on the tight curves. Allen had been chiding him from the back seat, like a mother sometimes trying to reason with him to slow down. I felt like a Marx Brothers extra, sliding onto Allen, and him to me. Allen managed to load his camera and take the famous shot of Neal looking at Anne under the torn headliner of the Pontiac.

We got to my friends house in Bolinas and Neal and Anne were being romantic again. Neal picked up a literary book and started reading dramatically from it. He sat reading while our host fixed some tasty guacamole. Just regular folks visiten...out picknikin...Allen like to be folksy and imagine what others might see.

I had a collage show at the Batman Gallery on Filmore St. Neal had been hanging out with a notorious speed freak. The amphetamine heads were not embraced by the psychedelic flower types. The only common thread that ran through them all was pot smoke. Neal had just come from the Goldwater convention at the Cow Palace. He was with another methhead and Neal wore a Republican straw hat and had a cane that helped his Gene Kelly swagger and wore a Goldwater for President pin. He may have leaned toward the Republican Party because it was Kerouac's party. Neal followed Kerouac in literary and political matters. I saw Neal later at a freedom of speech rally in Berkeley, taunting the protestors. Ginsberg immediately put his spin on it saying Neal was just acting like a crazy Buddhist. Neal usually ran with the desperadoes when he needed speed and was broken off with Anne, whose source may have been dry.

I went with Anne to the S.F.V.D. clinic, which was one of the city's more thriving, grand atavistic social clubs, and I overheard Anne confessing to the doctor that her "husband" was "promiscuous". I wondered to myself if the Doctor knew the understatement. Neal was always trying to put the make on any female, even mine, but I never knew how many people he was poking. There seem to be a catholic side to all of this, and Neal wanted to be a "good" lad. If you take away Aids, and violence against women, which were not issues in those times, Neal tried to be virtuous.

Neal was off and on with Anne. As the demand for Neal became more, he had to spread himself thinner. He had just return from a marathon drive he had wanted me to go on, talking it up at a previous party in Berkeley with Ginsberg and Kesey. Neal had it all planned out how we would stop in Wichita, my hometown. He went to N.Y. to see Kerouac and in record time was back in S.F. driving a '57-58 red and white

Dodge or Plymouth he had scored. He was panicked about something to do with his driver's license. He had, of course, been stopped somewhere. It was then I realized how fearful he was of the bureaucracy. I shared this fear but wasn't in his shape, so after his begging me, I went down to the California Motor Vehicles office with him. There might have been more to it, but Neal was terrified. Turns out it was just an insignificant detail like his signature or something, and he seemed relieved.

Karen Wright, my friend we had visited in Bolinas, brought a record to Gough St. She wanted Allen, Neal and Anne to hear it. Neither Neal nor Anne seemed to have time for music. Allen seemed unmoved, but interested when we listened to Bob Dylan for the first time.

Soon, visitors from Hollywood arrived, Dean Stockwell attended some poetry readings. There was a lot of traffic through the historic flat. Ginsberg had lived in this flat in the '50's and returned to it after a long stay in India, at just the moment the Hippies were at full tilt. Soon there were parties thrown for all the old garde, Ferlinghetti, and Don Allen and "anthology of poets," and the new garde, Leary, and of course the burst of the new sound of Rock and Roll. Ravi Shankar, whom some called the "Lawrence Welk of India," suddenly awakened in the heart of Rock' N Roll in the Renaissance Revival.

I had just sat down in the front room at 1403 Gough when Neal and John Bryan came running in. "Turn on the T.V. Charley, the President has been shot. We watch the news a while and agreed simultaneously like a room of ex-cons that Oswald was a Patsy. It was after a double consipiracy theory evolved, that would have had Oswald as a player. The ex-cons are usually right about such things. Gavin Arthur was quoted saying he voted for Nixon. Since Gavin was a known seer, astrologer, and from a political background, he had forecasted the assassination. That event pretty much ended the fun for a while. Little did we know, what cynicism had begun.

I was in City Lights one day and told Ferlinghetti that I was going down to a garage where the Merry Pranksters had parked their bus. He was uninterested. He only partied when a literary event was going on. He liked the salon more, where one could bang a tambourine and recall the expatiate canons. I bought a pair of driver's leather gloves for Neal. He was at the cockpit of the bus "FURTHER". Anne was nowhere in sight. There were lots of pretty girls and boys on the bus. Neal swung the door open and took me to meet Tom Wolfe who was standing by with Ken Kesey, ready for a trip.

I didn't hear much from Neal after we had spent a good Thanksgiving Day together: Neal, some of his friends, Allen, some of his, and my older sister and her husband Frank, with whom I worked on the docks. Anne helped prepare the meal. It was some years after that I visited Glenn Todd, who had stayed at Gough Street after we left. Some junky or souvenir hunter had torn off the front door. Glenn put up some crates and cardboard and stayed on. He scored big time, though. The redevelopment office gave him a great Victorian in a good neighborhood. I asked him if he ever saw Neal. He said "Yeah..Neal came around a few months ago, I made him some coffee. He looked gone in the face."

When Neal fell on the tracks in Mexico, he took the fall for a lot of us. We, who in the 50's (like now) abhorred conformity, liked some reefer, popped pills, drank and cruised, had a healthy distrust of the system we were part of, and put freedom above repression. Historically, we were really politically correct in that the system proved to have its own perpetual institutionalized criminally. Those outside the system always understood the police as an instrument of the state. Smoking reefer in a wholesome and tribal manner meant that you were real. You were a Johnson, not a Shit, to put it in a Burroughs' hobohemian phrase.

ROBBING
THE PILLARS

Philip Whalen, Charles Plymell, Allen Ginsberg, and Lawrence Ferlinghetti. San Francisco, 1963.

Charles Plymell and Don Faulkner, Wichita, Kansas, 1950,
Plymell's 1950 Oldsmobile convertible.

PROLOGUE

"Robbing the pillars" is a coal miner's saying. To close a mine, they knock out the supporting beams of the cave while exiting the opening. I think the phrase is a useful metaphor. Not only does it capture the age-old concept of crawling out of the cave towards light, but seems a fitting expression for the closing of this last decade of the century and the millennium that I call "The Age of Apostasy". In it contains the seeds of something we cannot yet see.

I chose the word "apostasy" to describe the milieu of Gen X. Having been a rebel through the 50's and 60's, I feel sympathetic and sad for a generation that is beginning to feel the squeeze of overpopulation in all its seminal horror. My generation ignored such problems in their quest for the American Dream. After the great wars, we could have created a real goodness in the human experience, but our altruism did not overcome the Cold War. No, we exhibited the same old greed and avarice—only now we contaminated and endangered all other species as well as our own and imposed the old moral progress on the stolen lands, a recipe for bad karma. As if in fictive plastic form, the spark of spirit extinguishes.

I hear this apostasy in the songs of the decade: "That's me on the corner/losing my religion. "Apostasy (in Latin from apostasia defection; from late Greek apostasis revolt) is defined as the "abandonment of one's religious faith, a political party, one's principles, or a cause." And why shouldn't the young defect? They know they have been schooled in hypocrisy, lies, injustice and unfairness, just as a few in my generation knew. In addition, they are brutalized by a toxic planet exploding violence and misplacing love. They sing about "revolushun."

The "insolence of office, law's delay" was around before Hamlet; throughout civilization we thought these undesirable traits could be corrected through our intellect: by learning ethics, civics, morals, etc. But always love, compassion and generous spirit were missing. True, the message flared briefly In the 60's, but it was squelched in favor of greed and materialistic corruption that served our intellect.

Add to that greed and materialism the mass of population and the toxicity caused by it, and there seems to be no way out. Of course philosophically the end is either now or later. In my lifetime most creative people recognized this, but even creativity was co-opted by Moloch. The system became Goya's Saturn, eating its children. Yet, a religious feeling lingers on the trigger finger of the big bang.

This section is dedicated to GEN X, the generation that includes my children. I had it good as a teenager in the 50's, and I wish them the best, even high on hell. An "old-money" millionaire once asked me why my poetry contains so much despair and anger. Change the world and I'll change my words.

This book is also dedicated to the Beat Generation and the Exiles who kept literature in the open, airing mainframed ideas in religion, politics, and values. Resigned to Love, to make it all cohere, Pound said as he closed up shop, "I have brought the great ball of crystal/who can lift it?" Many busted out young. Others influenced singers who died trying. Some became what they rebelled against. Others lived secretly playing the blues on their back porches.

The poetry in this section bridges the generation gap and hopes to inspire those rising to try to save the world. Only a cynic laughs at that! Carl Watson wrote that the only religion left is "Be Careful". In a world of accumulating complexities, I would not, as I once did, go looking for trouble. Life is difficult enough, now, even for those on their right path. The ones with their eyes open, with good air to breathe and good water to drink, must see that, although we carrying heavier loads of toxicity, fakery and propaganda for the people, by the people, we are not at the end but jumping into an immense historical change.

Cherry Valley, New York

TWO ALBANYS

In 1909 in Albany, NY
Carl Jung, marveling at the birth
of our technological culture,
observed: "All that is frightfully
costly and already carries
the germ of the end in itself."

William Burroughs spoke of "the devalued human stock."
Elmore James sang "I want to take you someplace you ought to be."
Tesla, hoping for peace said, "Electricity will annihilate space"
Hart Crane traveled down this valley,
marveled at the Utica train station,
alluded to the telegraph when he wrote:

"The last bear, shot drinking in the Dakotas
loped under wires that span the mountain stream.
Keen instruments, strung to a vast precision
Bind town to town and dream to ticking dream."

Samuel Morse wrote a code on this communication highway
known in his day as The Great Western Turnpike outside
the window of this old school on west to Buffalo, Toledo,
Chicago, where clacking Amtraks flash past cattle cars
ribbed eyed steel hysterical death vision light shuttered
along the savage rails and snow covered salvage yards to
slaughter like from the land of Custer, the Loser,
to the land of the Yellow Stone on west where the White Buffalo was
replaced with Ronald McDonald's plastic rotten death.
Where old news superbly respun into politically correct
new morality speak hypes and hawks the dying
empire in the electromagnetic torrents of toxic sunsets
more beautiful, more deadly than ever like the old day-glo tinctures
from the summer of love; old folks marvel at the colors
from their sun decks in late dead afternoons.
As far as the eye can see, Sioux City to far away Wyoming
via interstate dead banging wind to Pocatello, Idaho and lo
the Great Western Turnpike continues to Albany, Oregon,

and 60 miles west of that, an equivalent distance as
Cherry Valley is to Albany, NY appears the Pacific
and this century's last glance into its soul.
I SING PRAISES, Service for William Burroughs
A year ago, Lawrence. Kansas, August 6, 1997
The Muse is satiated, well paid
Her splayed wand, still sparking
Her stray cats all found a pillow
Her Nefarious boy came home
OSIRIS, share thy Throne
for the spirit lost in the fields and towns
and villages smoking through factories in Ohio
Debauch'd and Darkly Ag'd monoxide mutants
hills of trees piled like radioactive french fries
the air as thick as the melted plastic sunset.

Old Greek tragedies played in modern atone
At Coliseum's Blood Montage of metrodome
2000 years converge under Trump's Triumphant Towers
built on contaminated soil where Noise is Poverty.

The century falls like a garishly painted window
of the sweatshop loft where a poet digs in dumpster
warming his hands, mad as Kafka, flaming into
anger burning in the barrel fires on the Bowery,
his pants hanging below the cheeks of his ass.
I knew him well when flowers grew on upper sill.

His brother had to keep drivin' addicted to the wheel.
His sister has a shear-wind voice cold as a witch

Hard looker, mean hooker, commercialized vagina
Cum Laude from the Tattooed Neon School.
Deep heart, dark mind, charred to the cores
no longer has a name but a symbol for the last nights
became a stone from the common cemeteries rising
above each other's ring-pierced brow where
the wolf whistle tinged to tattered beauty.

The road map of gene-scrambled identities
along the streets of old visions of
young men from the towns arriving
at Psychedelic Heights with flashlights,
searching the street maps
in dark seats of Volkswagens.
Later to follow the Grateful Dead to martyr.
Keep the joy. Where's the harp? Where's the altar?
Where's Little Richard? Doncha' dump him in the gutta'
Hey mate, blade skate, off to school, or meditate
sense survival in information world where
weeping, seeping, sarcophagi in Chernobyl,
icons blowing in contaminated winds.

The age started at a boy's school in New Mexico
where a giant shovel dug into the Sacred Circle where
all remains of the paranoid radioactive reactive age will be
buried for millions of years beneath the leaking spirits
and demons that kept generations' minds
trapped in the cold war curtains.
What shaped thought do you peddle now?
Your paranoia pushes phoney drug propaganda
and your lies and newmoralityspeak dumb your young
whose only dream is honesty and who laugh
at bannering newspapers that print the pimp.
Poet, Priest, and President
took drugs, dropped acid, got laid, so
who in the hell is this big act for, anyway? The cows.

IN THE AGE OF APOSTASY
(this is the serious stuff, dude)

for Matt

Incense wafting like ghosts
Autumn,
and the days are numbered,
stored up in the attic, spiders of
singularity hanging by a thread

The young boys built a shrine
for one of their own
who rode off the highway
on a motorcycle, the girls

brought torn Pink Floyd tickets
the Bic lighters, and Camel butts
I know their shrine, I trembled when
He busted out for all of their glory

denied them in the memory of moan
while their fingers fold the wrappers
of the age into cryptic collages
they, inheritors of tinselly foiled trash

And dead images in the dynamo of cities
and towns and the society of lies they
take to bed with them, the TV screams
silent images in holocaust holograms

The idols and twisted morals and values
of goodness confounded in their schools
while grimm'd limb'd brutalized youngsters
born toxic, weave God's helix rug, sing revolushun
in overpopulated teen streets intersecting honest
pierced anger, their heart, a victim of eternal hoax.
There is a reason for the violence loss of morals, values,
in this Age of Apostasy, you killed their love
when they needed their world without lead in their blood
and the honesty and wisdom of the ages

floating down polluted turd-filled streams.
Their stars under surveillance
Zen commandments digitized
punks live in bandaged pads
wear slavery's socks from chain stores
fasten sunset's carnival light to
their doorway with crazy glue
and inhale the last generation's bad air.

Short pants to the ankles
baseball caps on backwards
standing, kicking, waiting

I have seen the tired souls
in silent gasp of anger and despair
try to grasp a memory of truth that
no one is created equal to what.

I chopped the sign
but it didn't stop the destiny.

FROM ANCIENT LAND (Vernal Equinox Dream)
Washington, D.C. 1984

They walked the sunrise, soul-burned travelers,
wearing hats tilted like Autumn's landscaped hills.
Rough-faced sailors, eyes laden like water rills
scanned the horizon till shorelined stars unfurled.

New wind in the air for those waft on the seas,
new smell of earth dug away to align the leys.
And they came forever wandering, as if set free
from cracks and rifts and vortices, as when some
great stone moves from its natural mortises; they
sailed the wind, a front of chaotic charges ignited,
careless in radiance, patterns of heaven unsighted.

(At 5:30 a.m. I awoke from a dream of Vernal Equinox
like a farmer called early for spring plowing, or a
driver with an early start knowing the aching miles
that stretch across the long heart of the prairie.)

In the Oklahoma Territory my father left his coffee pot
on the stove in his sod house, and he drove
cattle down to Galveston town. He saw the
lights beckoning on the port side of the bow,
headed for Italy, brought back a color picture
of the Isle of Capri, and when he returned the
next year, the coffee pot was in the same place.
And the picture for years was the only decor alone
in the farmhouse room askew from a rolling cyclone.
The wind, a terrible pitched-moan to stillness,
silent as trowels through the loess and grass.
Blowing dust through cracks of doors and windows,
sculpted the still waves day and night. The house
took in the wind of the wolves' howl, the song
of the coyote, and the long train whistle dragging
the reptile's whispering scream of time; the pioneer's
pitch of desperation, first loud then soft as the crimson sun
then distant into the stars where cowboys herded
the dark clouds out of the sky and sailors lined

the bow like star flung bodies, wanderers, happy
visitors who come when the new wind comes to
keep me half awake, half dreaming. . .so very many
where deep chasms of history gives dazzling narrow light

My father rode down through the equinox in a perfect
visioned dream as if he had never been away. I
wanted to show him the nation's capital, but he
was here on other business; he wanted to find his
merchant marine papers, why, I don't know, maybe
to show passage through eternity beyond cold space.

'Look at the beautiful masonry,' I said to him, 'look at
the Merchant Marine Building with its exquisite work
of brick and tile, and bronze doors, and frontispieces.'
We went down to a little section of the city by the sea.
'Oh,' I said to him, 'this is just like Italy.' The marble
and the little streets and the glassworks and the women
who walked there, the women he joked with, and the sailors,
and the bricklayers, and the carpenters, and threshers
like Kansas long ago, drifters passed in the street
recognized in memory, composite in chirality, patient
in formality; they, the blazed-faced, hand-hewn people
who walked the narrow streets by outdoor cafes.

He knew where to go, not up to the marbled entrance
but down a side street low, near a building, where,
in the dust of the sea bottom, beneath a small cupola
stood a woman by a counter of endless floating files.

'Draw me a picture of the last scene you remember
as a mariner,' she said. He drew a picture of himself
sitting on a bed, his sailor's hat cocked to one
side, a coffee cup on the table. He asked her jokingly,
'how do you want me, ma'am, hobbled and ironed?'
She helped him look. 'How far back?' He didn't know.
Down in the sea dust of a bottom drawer they found
his papers water stained brown. He pulled them out
and waved and yelled as if he had found passage
toward the wild fix of stars, or Isle of Capri.

TO A DEAD PIGEON: UNDER THE FREEWAYS

Dead pigeon lying in the street
with your ingrown tongue so stringy,
I don't have to stop here and look at you,
knowing that I have to write a poem for you,
and worst of all, only caring halfway
that you lie there in final arabesque.

You look like a bird pattern in a rug
only one dimension to the street.
An Eagle you are, I've seen on Indian stone,
you no longer go with choo-choo neck
and spaceman eyes.

Your form on the pavement will soon go away,
first the feathers blue and grey
and your pinions crushed.
Your delicate ribs.
And you say, "who should want my feathers."
It's not the feathers but the flying . . .
you see, caught in
physics! astronomy! oh that notions
could line on scale
with dumb coward glaze
begging voices from the wind you flew.

Myself wanting Venus and Mars
to crush into the dirt we die in,
closing the pyramid of light.
Oh long thin rotting muscles
that once breathed the secrets
of the family bird,
I want to give you ritual
but I'm afraid,
walking past the blind with tin cups.
Afraid I cannot pull out.
Afraid there is not reason long enough
to find my way home . . .
under the freeways.

HAND ON THE DOORKNOB

1900's have left me faded years, take 'em all
one hand on the doorknob, the other on the wall
so far away from home I can hear the old bull bawl
one hand on the doorknob the other starting to crawl.

The government gave themselves my money
every time I applied for a dream
And I heard the people scream
they are taking our rights away

I painted pictures to conceptualize
the careers post-modernists analyze
They all sounded the same
and had no sense of shame

If the economy is so damn good
how come they charged me double
Nothing but phonies under a hood
just wanting to make some trouble

Oh they called me a loser
but their sun leaves a yellow line
I should have been a boozer
and just paid a fine

February brought a runaway in the snow
to a strip mall like a hobo in Soho
his lament, nobody care

I put my hand on the doorknob
but didn't know if I was home
went into the correct world to find a job
a headhunter's chick just made me moan

A meth head farm worker peels off his Jesus
long ago picking a potato, his eyes and mind same
as a Detroit meat packer on metal and Methedrine
cutting as fast as I ever seen, blood and all

Corvette parked outside the mall, take it all
People ready for the end of the world, take it all

JANUARY

When Stars forget their faces,
and a closer look at nature becomes
cruel. Birds fly ashore in April
remembering their eggs in the sky.
Then I click like memory in birth
and death, and see the branch
and stream of law entwine.

The spider weaves haphazardly
forgetting the first part of the
spiral. Tired, perhaps, of the
trembling fly. But then the broken
web of frost becomes the ground
with unknown explorers with internal
sextant and shaky compass lined.
That is unfurled in vendor's empty
wares. What tracks unwind in radar
screen of all events. Lone wolf. A
warm slinking fact in film of life
around the earth. To cold frost town.

Tracks in the newly fallen snow over
vortex plains, cold misted trees
gnarled tough in their scale of years.
Scraggly arms that reach for moon.

As in a month the moon repeats its
fundamental note. Involuntary stomachs
drift to Venus . . . she repeats hers, and
within the baby yet another aspect opens.

Hungry wolf cannot see the beginnings of snow,
tracks over the mirror in the hungry wind of ice.
Secret atoms passed on and on in the howling wind.
(Home to unwind the mummy roll by roll?)

Is there a part of me, an edge I
cannot peer beyond, a hidden angle,
a side I cannot see, A ghost? But then?
Your admiration unfolds my face
with a river of peacocks across my brow,
a flutter of light years in my chest.
But what is applause when drama closes?

MANSIONS

Am I delivered unto these old doors
where keyholes are too large,
and good-bye letters lie askew
under smelly windowpanes?

I heavy step the wino stairs
of phantom murderers,
while an ancient line of ghosts
walk up my eyes to peep.

And O that breath of sleep
I have at night,
crossing over hills of prairie hay
where early frost stigmata
bears the light.

Like in a western movie
I run in the hills
leap over the rocks and stones
carved in their time there.

Hiding in crevasses
I drew the smoke from outlaw guns,
some fun there, dying on the run.

How I climbed
with my Winchester in my hand,
chasing Einstein, shouting
questions with a Kansas twang.

How like a movie
dreams ago,
in which I fell asleep,
awoke after everyone had gone
and tugged my wraps around me
to go home alone.

O thou ancient, lucky warriors,
with your enemy in front of you,
how will thy bow and gun
and arrow fend now,
in a Winchester Mansion,
with every window to a subdivision home.

(Inspired by the Winchester Mystery House in Santa Clara Co., CA)

STAR TATTOO DYING ON THE DAY-GLO

i

Star tattoo
shining
on a billion cars tonight,
      metal gone mad,
      polluted curb upon a cement globe,
carried to a grave and cement slab.
Stupid man so close to destruction,
      not yet divine
      thinking by power
in line of Cheap bondage
      waiting at the stoplight
      beneath my window
lost in fumes.
Metal mind
kept in misery, taxed
kept waiting
      waiting at the stoplight
      beneath my window.
A Man-burned mind
      not wanting that but metal
      metal with no God
      women with metal bodies
      metal with no heart
      metal worshiped savior,
      sculpture on church

to say nothing of soul.

Rich man's dole, little man's pride.
The little men against themselves,
      in deficit
trespassing on the big man's world.
Make the little man march
make the little man hate
make the little man kill.
Will you rise before this festival now
while the visionary holds his mind in place?

Under the circus tent he alone can see
the darkest thread of night
       tincture of sun
Bodies mining the purple
      gold skin shivers against the horizon.

Do you remember the dance
under the fur medicine ball
      we danced
      did rituals as
          if gathering amber
     naked by the fire?
In Hollywood, Woodstock, now.

Hail Gypsy moth antennae!
Rimbaud Arabian Nights of "The Doors."
Fecundity of American mind and American meadow.

ii

Will you arise from
      "the Day-Glo Ganges"
      "the slime of festival abandoned"

stolen from Life.

Inherited memories silently echoing
radio over the states
playing to the sharp young men
      who used to command the future,
Kennedy news melting in Linotype lead.

     Will the ladies
     who push Watchtower
     think the kingdom is at hand?
As they who have witnessed Jehovah
must now witness Woodstock.
     (And at dawn they journeyed
     to the festival of Bethel
     and at evening they arose

and left.)
Back to the asphalt.
    Crawling into
        Electric vision, a franchise.

iii

Bodies that move
        in numbers larger than
        armies of ancients
        seen bivouacked on the
horizon.
Flashes of alchemy
in the pilgrimage
numbered more than armies of old
                they have suffered
                as the downtrodden
and felt the policeman's stick
they have seen the eyes of old patriots
        with no place to go
        but the street
otherwise they trespass on the masters' soil.
They have seen puppets placed in high places
they have been ordered to leave their assemblies
        or be made into criminals.

But the right to free speech
        Is as strong as the constitution
and freedom to gather

iv

Puppets in the White House
put their own boys in power.

So true a lesson in any grade B movie.
        "The likes of you and
        me, sailor, are just ballast,"
words recalled of my father on the high seas long ago.

Come over here, Bud, and
live off another's toil.

Back in San Francisco
the men on the dock
    say the Pope is fruit
    and the Mafia owns the company.
And the men respect
each other
because they demand
        their piece of the pie.

v

On Charles St., Baltimore,
a black couple handed us a pass
to hear Dizzy Gillespie.
        He signed my notebook
in a blue rose room
of Arabian nights
costumes of silk
gold rings
and gold watches
           gold labels on whiskey
           and gold women.
A Sunday afternoon concert
like long ago
when things were smooth and groovy.
           Not like West Coast
           body thing—
           East Coast is heart
           and head.

And in sweet memory again to 1950's
I hear King Pleasure jumping
with my man Sid from the city.
Dakota Stanton swinging
When Sunny Gets Blue.
Baltimore Oriole, Annie Ross
    I say, lapsing into memory.

Or if I want chop suey
I go to St. Louie.
I love you, Peggy Sue; but
more so, Peggy Lee.
You see I like
to recall the 50's
would like to feel
the emotions of the 40's
perhaps a love affair in the 30's
Paris in the 20's
or kicks in the 60's.

vi

Whenever you go to Elko
and that's in Nevada, of course,
check in at a motel and turn on the tube
Channel 8 at 3 o'clock—
image extending in space
above the lone wolf cry.
Transmission god
tower of the prairie
organ brain controller
of the re-uptake pump
above the star shaped ganglion
stalking the nerves of a desert child.
Spare parent of beautiful children
O speak of this we are in
what is it and where does it end?
And slowly the words
with soft background music
float by:
RANGE FIRE TODAY
then comes the RAINFALL IN INCHES
WIND DIRECTION
WIND VELOCITY
BAROMETRIC PRESSURE
then comes the TEMPERATURE IN FAHRENHEIT
THE RELATIVE HUMIDITY
TIME LSD
T.V. PIX, INC., ELKO, NEV.

BOWERY BUMS, NYC, 1969

I see their tattered faces changing in the flame
above the barrel fires burning on the Bowery.

torment of their souls paints pictures strange
poetry pressed in the pavement resembling coins.

Their song the wailing sirens of the night,
their hearts burned out in barrel fires
where big trucks beat the pavement day and night.

They roam the streets like orators
making ragged gestures in the wind.

Julius Caesar...Hamlet....Robin Hood!

REMEMBERING RICHARD BRAUTIGAN

That's Reba, Richard
you know, the kid
who arrived with flowers in her hair
At the Greyhound station
go 69'ers from the senior class
across the land of coffee-tonk cafes
with hard neon illuminating bacon and eggs
grabbed her bags from the locker
headed for the baths at Big Sur
via the head shop in the Haight.

Reba's name written wildly where
cameramen cowboy oracles ride
Reba ready
Reba right on
Reba rid of speed
Reba ready hip
Reba arriba arriba
Reba rich girl reading
Richard Brautigan on the beach
Reba tough
Reba together
Reba danced with Joan Baez
Hey that's my bag
Reba pop rock art
Reba wrote a poem for Allen Ginsberg
Reba saw Brautigan naked at the end party
Reba coke collage digs dope dancing
from Filmore West to Filmore East.

Scratch your name on East Village brick
and let your belly shine
your breasts still pure from the Big Sur baths
the Pacific's spray of Saturn and Sun
where the air pierced your pores and tongues
Redwood lips bursting with rapture.
News shops hawk reality of The Morning Sun
of faded type, Berkeley, to buy a gun

to blow the windows out of time
watch the tanks all in a line
troops on the roof ready and aim.

(She packed her long dresses
and threw the I Ching,
drove over the bridge in a limousine.)

GIANT

for James Dean

Wanna fight,
wanna race up the grapevine?

We knew the cause—
the socks didn't match—
and by now
all life's neater memories.

Bye, Bye, Mrs. Mildew
we all have to go now—
enjoyed the pie.

Goodbye, Monsieur Dog,
Goodbye, Jet Rink,
Goodbye, Giant.

TOXIC WASTE
for Jack Micheline

Kinfolks spin tales into rugs while
Jack Micheline weeps shirts flapping
in the wind of unfinished seams.

On train from the Bronx, take it all
Fort Apache, it's all I got, take it all

Crooked tent
sign of lazy fellow
battery dead like last night's Ford

Genius . . . glue that holds all things together
Logic. . . bonded science to burst its last particle.

Progress settles like chain-linked puked plastic
all over the sky's expensive mirror . . .

Jack Micheline is on his way

A twin tornado becomes drunken
clowns at the carnival on stilts way up
near the Big Top.

Now the foam swells in the river
feet sewn into refuse like pillows at a craft fair,
but the wind has one eye and carries a knife.

Jack Micheline on Van Ness at Market

We connect the tempting telepathic plasma
of truth like a little spider, or a rider, hurrying in the night
to get food to its shelter where more mouths wait.

Jack Micheline saw it all

The crow struts around like a dude on the hard white snow.
Under the cold wolf moon we poison our environment
and want each other silently while exchanging a video.

NAMES I'VE LEARNED
for Catfish

Einstein, our modern oracle
spoke in equations rhetorical.
Afterwards, the nuclear claw
dredged energy from sacred maw.

Ray Charles witnessed the rolling scene
when earth turns faster, everything leans.
We of the earth have a sunflower's brain
yearning from the seed echoed in grain.

Loren Eiseley kicked a puffball irresponsibly,
used creativity to ward off melancholy;
hopped a freight dragging bones and twine,
left his faithful dog in a lonesome whine.

Little Richard rose through hot sauce and digs
the Rosey Finger'd Dawn and sticky finger'd ribs.
His bright-eyed songs fed his black angel soul
until the sirens outside his window let him go.

George Jones drank up his spirit light that shines,
in motels' shattered mirrored pieces of his mind.
He has probably never read what Emerson bade,
that there's a crack in everything God has made.

Lewis Thomas implied we might only be.. uh,
by-products of photosynthesis and mitochondria.
Ideas! Bruno was burned at the stake for less
but we have our God to lift us from the mess.

Ask James Watt, a brain by itself, removed no less,
from natural wilderness of unknown purposes;
who'd leave the scene of the genetic accident forsaken
to save his skin on roads where more beasts are taken.

Reagan knows our money tics feed on warm blood
and baby boomers now jog in exhausts of Firebirds.
He wants the old films rerun because he's an actor
he'd have Science study Freedom as a risk factor.

RAPID RONNIE RAP BACK JIVE KANSAS 1955

Doc Moonlight bought a brand new T-bird from writing scripts
Amphetamines drove fast hard bodies over the high steppes
Fifty year' ago his daddy bought a mare in Dodge City
Wyatt Earp's grandson now sells new cars in Wichititty

Life on the high plains, borrowed on a pile of loans,
I drove; Ronnie handed me Pound's Selected Poems.
Outside Zip's Club we smoked and pissed
inside, Pack Rat picked his bass in bliss
his eyes rolled back, in closed fret
scoo bop to do, de bip bip, from hep
to hip, to hop, be de bop . . . next set
like cat cartoon characters boing back.
Swiinnging man, on an astrological star
his nose inhalers packed behind the bar
candy-wrapper's cosmos and benzedrine
dragnet, luncheonette, make the scene,
play it straight, if fate . . . says best
really bad, half sad, oh fay, oh say,
shuffle on down slide away from the mass
wanna smiz zoke a jiz zoint of griz zass?

Rapid Robert Ronnie Rasmutin Rannamuck

Thief, pimp, artist, hood
alias Barbital Bob—stood
under the neon of Zip's Club.
His subterranean bellhop's boyhood forays
met Kansas Big Intersection's wild mores.
By light from the stained glass windows
he sketched pictures between the shows.
Illuminated in gold-faced fading stories
he saw his dreams flyspecked with glory.
He stuffed his pockets with dope and dates of whores
while he gazed too far beyond the gayly painted doors.

Rapid Ronnie rides the moonlight high
Pack Rat scoffed pills and played melodic
drank Oxybiotic that made him neurotic

Jimmy Mammy, just outta the joint, heard
Big Indian was gonna steal Doc's Thunderbird.
Ronnie went along, reciting Pound's verse
riding the terrible crossroads of the universe.

Big Indian let out a yell of centuries of pain
drove into the Bulldog's* tractor-trailer lane.
Jimmy Mammy broke his jaw and lay in years of highs
Ronnie grew old and secret under California skies.

Big Indian lay dead, his eyes confused
staring at the heavens . . . forever wider
than his moon's new earth that refused
him shelter from the great white spider.

*Robert Branaman married Sue Mack, debutante of Los
Angeles. (Mack Trucks/ Bulldog hood ornaments). In San
Francisco they were intimates of Billy Jharmark (Billy Batman/
Batman Gallery) and others of the 60's S.F. Renaissance. They
lived in Big Sur and at one time in a '52 Chevy on the streets
of S.F. They had three children. His son, an actor, first
appeared with Robert and his paintings in a cameo in The
Doors movie. His older daughter became a leading fashion
model in L.A. Susan died of cancer at an early age.

*This poem is about experiences and language of the 50's
before "Hip-Hop" and before the author had heard of the
Beat Generation.*

HOLLYWOOD BLVD.
For Dean Stockwell

In Hollywood aged poodles recoil in fright.
Ancient sorority queens, chew Juicy Fruit
in Topanga Canyon all night.
Hitchhikers from eternity flag your Chevrolet
and hug your Blue Jeans in Barney's Beanery
where they've added another room to hell
the jukebox keeps repeating
"Second Hand Rose".
And in unison towards the sunset of
Santa Monica beach
a thousand long fingers
of high school sweethearts
hold their cigarettes
through wisps of smoke.

There is a chance,
Second Hand Rose,
a star may fall at your feet.
But you know that chance
withers your lips as you sing
many versions of your love poem
torn alone in pages of the night's
tarnished wings of the Angel's Flight.
Past Fante's all the way up Sunset Strip
as unlikely as Dante finding self help programs
in heaven the lights of Los Angeles
endlessly hang like
a hustler's mad beads.

Cast this spell on neon
dye tonight, dark moon,

for tomorrow that ounce
of stardust will be
wiped from Cadillac chrome
unnoticed by freeway hawks.

(April 1968)

KINDERGARTEN LESSONS

A wistful blonde from kindergarten class
came calling on Billy one day.
He ran downstairs and hopped on his bike
(which still had training wheels)
Look at me! Look at me! I can pop a wheelie!
They chased each other round and round.

His rivals from across the way came to play
But he and she played with each other true
and the poet knew how to listened that day
Na na boo boo, stick your head in doo doo.

Now son, you must come inside
for some appreciation in art.

Let's look at some Magritte pictures.
...

They can't build a man out of rock, can they?
...

A real funny one I think
I see birds in the cage
and one out of it
the man is holding a stick
he's sitting on a mound of sand
he has no eyes, no mouth, no nose,
no hair, stomach or elbows.
He has a cape, a hat and a bag
weeds are in back of him, and the sky.
The cage is open, that's why
the bird is out.
It came from the cage
in his stomach.
He's thinking about the birds.
...

The white bird out of a man's
stomach flew in front of
his face so he won't see
...

A house is in another house
a house with an open window
it looks so far
it looks so neat.
...

I never saw an apple like this
up to the ceiling!
It could go in my room
I'd eat my way in
That could be my room from now on.
...

Boobies, a ball, a bellybutton,
penis hair, butt butt, and hand
on the butt where the butt sticks out
where the stripe is!
....

Snow in the head of an eagle
in the beak and on the eye
and the mountains and the
clouds are glass broken with
the eagle still on it.
...

Curtains and wood, glass broken
and the sun still on the glass
what's out in the sky
because it got painted on.

SAN FRANCISCO 1963
with Allen G. & Cassady

At the corner of Post St., and Gough
a chinaman has a store called
the Golden West Market.

The government plans to tear it down.
They're crooks he says.
Where I flind another place for store.

And next door there is a flat
which has stored past lives
in old baggage left by those
who saw too far behind
that pearly painted door.

I can see Neal now
feverishly unloading
old boxes of clothes, books, belts, etc.
And Justin smiling with his arms
outstretched in JOY!
Five years later, an institution.

And just this day
you return to Gough St.
As saintly now as ever
Chaplinesque down the sidewalk.

You bring some tapes of
Ezra, and I recall
that brain in a beacon
an eagle's eye wrinkled in stone.

That sculptured old man
alone with his muse.
Clarity of light years
wrecked in focused glory
of the unfit and unbroken.

Pound is still alive,
he's eighty-two you say.
Then you run around the
corner, your hair bouncing up and down.

The pawnbroker
of all unredeemed problems
of the worst of all possible worlds.

And I recall your gentle ways
when many lives were crossed upon
and set in mind of thee.

And the young burst forth untended;
blazing trails in long limousines.

Long-haired boys run past the house,
to the Avalon Ballroom scenes.

Popping their eternity
they run past the door
their rock and roll boots
more run over than before.
They are the young
you seek, but only speak
in whispers the long hallway.

The back door by the tumbling stairs
where Neal returned not long ago.
(Elephants, when ready, go
to their burial place.)
Where Betty and Frank slept off
cold alcoholic nightmares,
a slim thread of home to them all.
Maggie's wash now flaps between
the tree and dark lawn.

Clouds crash, eclipse
high above the jeweled ships
where a suburban

housewife's orange peels
went insane among
coffee grounds and bones.

Sailors of unrest
let the torch of amber
crawl on the door.

Pieces of life on that shady sea
feed back into files of eternity.

The young run past the door
with magic in their hearts.

"A cantankerous judge of men"
 You sternly say.

"Things are at a drag end," he said
one hand on the door knob.

CHERRY VALLEY 1974

When the day came back to me
I loved it
Elizabeth

Hot star over the river
The ring shaped like hydrogen
Over the line of sight
The window but a wavelength
And the light around the night
The village blends when lights go on
Into the sunset the hand connects
A game for winter nights from point to point

When icicles sprang in remote rotation
From the spring tooth harrow set some winters
Plow gears worn in their own alignment
Walking John came over the hill
Ed the Hermit honks past

And over the sleepy hollow moon
Lay superhighways monolithic ribbon
A ton of gravity under poured stone
Where workers leaned to a structured plan
Engineers saw nerves in their own bindings
Some future civilization will observe

And I sleep like old Rip Van . . .
The bowling alley across the street.

BALTIMORE ECLIPSE
for Phil Scalia

Did you see the sun blotted from the sky?
Like when the world ends and your hands
get cold and old women look witchy
and tell you strange tales. . . .
Did you see strangers arrive in a
field of straw and ice to warm
of the theft of the sun?
Who walks there with an idiot grin?
Who's that, and that, and that
who have no feathers nor shadows
when evening is two in the afternoon.
(Total over Virginia Beach and Edgar Cayce.)
I felt the ozone change.
The cobalt door creaked open
Noon was threatened.
Who may have crouched there, crouched there
before . . . unaware of cosmic superimposition.
Who was caught there, was caught there now
in the phantom's solid stare. Tell me
This is no sneak preview of things
lost in the garden of remembrance
where guards are stripped of their armor.
I saw the fairy tale stare painted on
doll's eyes of the wired man, flashing blue,
flashing blue, fixed on burning eels
swimming through the aether and grey
lads from Beatles movies in an invisible aquarium.
But oh that sheen and dust of gold;
Oh that crisp acetylene evening,
the city awash with purple, and
birds folding their wings in afternoon.
The hour Poe arose from his statue
over there, and walked around.
I saw his musty hair fall to his shoulder,
he stopped there to see his fellow
statues on the totem-slope of time
admiring their wings and horses.
Now down hill to reclaim his statue.

SHADES OF SAN FRANCISCO

Polk Gulch Cowboys roam rough-trade streets in Juke Patrol
under high plateaus where witchy Eucalyptus trees hold dark
secrets like starry-eyed Pachucos dreaming in the fog.
Two trees . . . where Mammy Pleasant picked brains from
banker husband.

It's now the Green Eye Hospital where ebony streetwalkers in
black leather and cheap moonlight bathe their wombs, as sweet
as Nubian princesses languishing under street lamp fur of neon.
Spells of laughter, and wanta date mister? In dress of green

they speak of the fallen woman, but oh the fallen man
tilted thighs and abrupt nipples . . . there in that old pad
to be torn down. . . . A bed of curtains and suede coat therein.

The long arms adorned with scars beneath bracelets of gold
and foreheads with burn marks of sweet vanity of youth.
Smell of hickory smoke deep into the night. Lonely fashion
ads torn and crumpled in leaves among wine bottles of lust.

My sister burns in that Chinese lantern of the Western Moon.

NOT A REGULAR KANSAS SERMON
for my mother in the hospital

Your grandmother married out of
the Trail of Tears.
You were born to a trail of fears,
a soddy, your brother dead.
Now you mistake me for him.

Then came the dust storms.
You put wet wash rags
over our faces so we could breathe.
Many women went mad, "God's Wrath"
in the storms, miles from anywhere.
It took strength, courage and prayer.
You shot jackrabbits to feed five kids
and even fed hoboes from the tracks.

You gathered cactus for us to eat.
(I saw some at a gourmet market in D.C.)
I've yet to see snow ice cream
or mayonnaise & sugar sandwiches.
I did see fry bread recently
at Harbor Place in Baltimore.

During the war you built airplanes
continued to do so until old age.
In a California hospital
a heart attack, you barely remember me.

Due to recent cuts in health care,
you have to leave the hospital in
two weeks, no matter what your condition. Eviction . . .
few rest homes take Alzheimer patients.
Perhaps things are best forgotten.

But it is difficult to think of you
who always supported yourself,
raised your children, worked the fields,
cooked the meals, did the wash,
survived the Dust Bowl,
made it through the Depression,
riveted airplanes for the war,

worked until management laid you off
to make room for "strong young boys."
(There were no women's rights.)

Out the door always. Used up.
Then out the door at the hospital
in two weeks—a rule—due to cuts.
There must be a lesson in all of this
but I'm afraid to say it.
What we can see, really, is that we're not equal.
The President could stay
in the hospital forever if he needed.
And so could most of those in government
who are provided for with the tax
deducted from your life's weekly checks.
Helped pay for underground bunkers that stay
vacant in the hills of Maryland and Virginia
for fleeing officials in an emergency. (Evict them.)
Then they wonder why there's an underground militia.
The Dalton Gang hideout is nothing compared to this.

We are really not equal in anything,
In sickness or dying unless
we've done what we've supposed to do
to make the country work for us. (Support them.)
You have to take always
to make sure you have yours
Adjustments for right or wrong
to be tendered at face value,
no matter how, from whom, or what.

If you don't want to take your
piece of the pie you're not good
unless you hoard it, no matter
how many die of hunger in the world.
Your taxes were also taken to
buy and store 2 billion dollars
worth of hoard, of milk and rotting
cheese in great Missouri caves.

Jesse James was small time compared to this.

SOME DAY THEY'LL COME AND CRATE ME
for Robert Peters

The Modigliani Show, National Gallery
Washington, D. C. January, 1984

I never knew there were so many
Bohemians, and not just any,
Pressed into the gallery that day.
Surely not the average goers they.
Beautiful people aging under their berets
Young, not so young, from sidewalk cafes.
Walking in Washington's cultural monolith
In leather jacket's hard punk make-up kits.
Hats of all kinds, dark glasses and beads.
Paint splattered pants worn at the knees.

Overalls, sneakers, and Mexican huaraches.
Jumpsuits, tweed coats, sweatshirts, no bras,
Camouflaged jackets—not allowed: barefeet.
Smoking pipes—even Ceci n'est pas une pipe
A Rimbaud parade . . . though a little heady. . . ,
I won't say, "I've known them all, already."
Last minute wardrobes, scarves in the breeze
Long cigarettes burned over wine and cheese.

Art America came to see
This exhibit of Modigliani.
But who is wrapped in a last review
Sleeps on Independence Avenue.
His biggest fear the beepers
And motorized street sweepers.
At the door I point to his head
And ask the guard if he's dead.
No, he says, not really . . , he
Sleeps on the grates, you see,
Otherwise his flesh may freeze.

His belongings were rotten feathers.
His bed old pillows and rags
Army blankets tethered with bags.
I asked if he was all right
He looked at me in fright.

What do you feel in your heart
About these patrons of the arts?

Oh them . . . let me tell you boy.
In his face I saw my eventuality
Ears lobes long replacing sexuality
Hairs sprouting from the nose escaping
Like nature's terribly brushed painting.

Rembrandt wrinkled and wild, he growled,
I used to work at MOMA's, and very loud,
Ya know what I mean, bud-dy?
Museum of Modern Art in New York Siddy.

I was a guard there—you catch the rift
Worked on the graveyard shift
Under those paintings I used to sleep
Just like here on this hard street
It was at night, you see,
Nothing but them and me.
In the empty museum
Along about three a.m.

Rooms full of masterpieces
I used to go to pieces.
Sculptures would appear
In dim light to my rear.
I talked to the paintings
Made love to them, y'know
Soon left new lines on Picasso
A few more dots on Seurat.
But I fell in love especially
With the nudes of Modigliani.
I kissed them in all the good places
Added pubic hairs, kissed their faces.
So now I'm part of the show!
My loves will outlast me, I know.
Though my time is spent
On the cold cement where no one touches me
I share that with them, you see.

IN MEMORY OF MY FATHER

To you who sung the riddles of that desolate Atlantis
while wind worn wagons swept a sunken trail into eternal dust.
To your sod, your grass, your easy hills of flint from glacial
slope to wanderlust. "Perfect cattle country . . . the best I've
seen since Uruguay." I'd oft heard you say, your dreams and maps
unfolded beneath those eyes that inventoried skies and knew
the winter owl's alarm where black beasts of Angus grazed?
I could not see as far, but went my way, you understood, and
watched the windmills tell their listless joy to silt and seam.
Life must be beautiful or all is lost . . . those bison of the clouds
were pushed from life . . . slaughtered for sport . . . now they are
the storm clouds watching us from eternity and far beyond.

And I did not know (when you showed me the lilies on the
limestone.) No . . . I did not notice you had grown old, your
hair had turned to silver . . . for I never thought you'd die.
I thought when this would end we'd all join hands together
like you told the babes at playtime long ago (that you hoped
we'd all meet in Heaven) in that dust bowl depression of Kansas.
It is hard to notice age in those who dream. You knew,
dreams are like youth, without them the world could not continue.
They are like the trees you always planted on sun-parched steppe,
enjoyed by those who pause and dream beneath the steel of time.
O fading America! Where is Thy promise! 0 catastrophic land!
This land you loved when newborn calf kicked up its legs. ..
you said everything wants to live . . . and expresses it.

The slap, slap, slap of tires on the grey concrete.
The tears on the way to the funeral. The biggest sky in Kansas.
"Wish I could find that old house where Grandmother lived,"
someone said, trying not to think, or feel, or sob.
You had told me you "might kick off" one of these days,
but I could never see you anywhere but waiting for us
on the porch, arms folded always with finger prop't
against sunburned cheek, Stetson tipped back, calm grey
eyes anxious and kind through smoke of neglected cigarette.
Home for Christmas in a few short days with newborn babe.
Giant cranes along the ditch . . . steel helmet'd
construction workers laying concrete pipe beyond all

of the Family Store T.G. & Y. or the old folks home you cussed.
Under vast space you saw the end products of wasted soul & hand
You saw the time begin to change, you saw the Atom Bomb.
You knew the true nature, foresaw the greed and plastic goods.
Saw those old jaws of monster oil wells pumping the never ending
depletion allowance of blood of man and earth.
"The little man pays the taxes."
And you sensed the vacant stare in faces. You saw man change.
You saw him buy on time. But he had no time to talk now. No time.
No time. Car tires squeal on nowhere road to make a time payment.

Skull of memory, how will your lamp burn now?
How will the dust, like pages scorch that canopy of bone?
How will those eyes rest against the dark storm of tears now,
when ozone rests on sage, calming that stampede of time?
It was the day of mustangs, the day a train whistle screamed that
Rockies' grade, when double header highballed and howled past
diesel trucks, water towers of unknown towns; soliloquy of
settlements and cemeteries beyond truck stops and salvage yard.

It was said you payed the ambulance driver before you let him go.
You dug some bills out of your old leather purse to hand him.
Through your hard span of life, you settled up so quietly
no one ever thought of you carefully.
They didn't care for unknown sages in unknown towns.
The end of a man, an age. I neglected to hug or kiss.

I was coming to see you from school, bringing my family.
Your father died with the fence unmended, the calves got out,
he didn't feel like riding; waited for you to come from school.
Everything changes but the meaning, and the tenderness passed on.
I stand here beside the peaceful grave, I stand here on earth
for the first time without you by me;
I take this land upon my shoulders.
The grain elevator over there is filled with wheat, the seed of
newborn day. The green Spring wheat. I am a father now. I know.
Your folks from Indiana came overland in covered wagons
crossed the Muddy at Hannibal Mo. , Mark Twain was 36.
To Belle Plaine and on to "No Man's Land." You staked your
claim. I remember the joke about no birth certificate, and
how the neighbors were healthy because they had government jobs.
Charley Dumbell shot himself with a Colt .45. You told the kids

wild stories, listened to Joan Baez, your favorite, with teenage kids.
You were always young and built the fence for your daughter's horse.
Lifting beams bigger than railroad ties. . .against the doctor's orders.
Post hole diggers left in the holes of prairie sod never used again.

Charles Plymell, Douglas Avenue, Wichita, Kansas, 1952.

1950'S BENZEDRINE HOBOHEMIAN VERSE
for Pat O'Connor

Sam Shusterman, the shoe store man, under the overpass in Wichita, cast iron front store if I remember right, touch of the Bowery, ya might say, sold dem used shoes to de old folk, poor folks and dos hipsters bopping down de street on de lower main drag, hip to de tip, a few blocks from the Great White Way snooker hall—- long time gone. He gots da used store where Florsheims shines and de floor shines too. Togs dat climb de frame. Wingtips, hightops, blues swedes too. Off-size, replete, repaired, recast, retread, rebuffed, runover, factory rejects.

He stretches the off size, puts Sholls's in de too-wides. Black and white shoes for blacks and whites. Pointy toes too for those with a point of view pegged pachuco trousers, oh silver watch chain deja vu.

High cowboy boots for shit stompers and whammied out galloping sluts. Hip boots laced in place, glittering fast socks sing. Plastic pumps wid taps on de heels, patent leather, gators galore.

I'm going down to Sam Shusterman's across the Santa Fe tracks and get me something to bop the night train, rack back my sack and park my nod in the sod. Konk it and fonk it but don't honk it, 'cause I gots my new used kickers on, shufflin' into town on my sneaker's shoestring—be kind to old Hobohemians, to hell wit' Doc Martins.

CHARLES HENRI FORD'S LAST PRINTS

Atlas on this star-studded Montauk
Beach, bleached night of dead cartilage
rotting haunting puzzles to their core.
Straddle night's space glazed with numbered
stars each to each pebble on the shore.

If you stand and throw your great knife
and cut an imaginary line through the
night sky, it is said that space is
so vast that no star would be hit.

Surrealism's magic master, beachcomber, leaves
lines like Spiderman's spit on skyscrapers
Gotham's duo, Batman, Robin and the rest.
Where Montauk descendants sell tobacco.

Leave your signals for a physicist to predict
and keyboard specialist to plunder the growing
algebraic garden of poppies, not having heard
such names as Tanguy, or Charles Henri, who,
before computers, had seen fractal patterns
curl back upon themselves as clean and easy
as a cut through space, a thread in Persian rugs,
or Seahorse dance in pride from deep ocean's ridge.

The course lives in the dance, in footprints, or
in the throne of worlds, the gnomon, Osiris sits upon.
Myth and geometry meet in the mouth and in the maw,
or in carcass washed ashore where upon he sits in
quick poppy's charm, in the kitchen's lost creations
raw food in the salons now gone, no more fine blade
slicing symmetry of the seed, or chopping herbs.
Latex oozing from the night, like a field of
Milky Way's frozen eternal footsteps above 72nd St.

The space time sung anew, like the canaries do, and
be bop too, to save their memories' weight for flight.

The brain lightens and ideas are boats untied
left in the currents of neurons,
less fantasized postulates school kids study
while long bladed orbits assassinate lovers
when the bare-light bulb moon dims the sun's room
unexplained, resonating, unscrewed, unfurnished with
the future by transient vestal vacancies of the past.
Sing for us, play for us, pray for our minimalist souls
while we sit in Acuras watching manipulators
coasting in Manhattan on roller blades of black ice.

GOD'S SWAP MEET
for Grant and Laki on the road

We live in a place
massacred by hostile tribes
toxic-brained and cruel
killers in a Victor Mature movie
alive again to lead the charge of skeletons
oblivious to what's around them.

Drove them west
You killed them once
in the lovely Kansas valley
that took their name

You stripped them of innocence
the way a stripping machine takes flesh.

An ad in the Sunday Pennysaver
Under the heading RECREATION:
FOR SALE: Mink or small animal skinning
machine and fleshing machine
both $750 Call 607 Garage Rat

"No matter how many houses you have built,
no matter how many people like you...
we had our lodges at the foot
of the hill, a pleasant tree-lined creek."

They took the lands of ancient seas
Took Creation, as divine right
But what God would have them

Trapped gods gnawing their bones
behind the bullet-proof glass
haunt those who left town
down the dark city streets
in the darkly crowded age.
Music beyond
the lighted avenue.

IN A WORLD MOVING SO FAST
ITS SYMBOLS ARE CRUMBLING

Bliss,
you're tricky,
going in and out of worlds.

That's why the better you do in this
dream the easier it will be down the line.
Or even now, to sing a new song of the heart
and avoid those things you hear on the street.

Be introspective and
light your own January!

Mr. Bazaar
didn't get far, but
his Pops bought him a steel guitar.

Petite panderer
Lower East Side
"I saw the unreality of it all"

Passerby spoke
and said
"Find your own reality."

Approaching magic marker faces
in San Francisco fog
which do not speak.
They avoid my eyes
in the Orient city.

Outside Buffalo snow
N.Y.C. train on savage rails
startled cattle eyes
in the train cars
passing close staying

fast hysterical death
through steel ribbed freight cars
glazed eyeballs, fiery white teeth
urban/suburban/sermon/burden.
Tunnel entrance
Hoboken
Who in the hell planned these roads
Janine, pointing to the
monolithic highway
where she hitchhiked
into the city.
Are we civilized yet?
Whose patsy now?
Far from honky-tonk angels.

FOUR SONGS
for Tony Moffeit

1.
Press "one" if you want to be right
Press "two" if you understand life
Press "dos" if you speak Spanish
Remain on hold if you want to commit suicide

2.
For every unmatched star that
breeds and dies along its beads
there is a creature in the woods
there is the season of ancestors
who found the ancient turtle
by the rocks along the Mohawk

3.
Pete seat mate has hat head on backwards.
His face becomes a high balloon
that jazzmen sing along with
when the uptake pump jumps
down in the planet's ballroom.
He struggles with a joint
and watches the fly fly away
zig-zag journey bangs against
the sunrise like the Emperor's gong.

4.
I've traveled around these states
like a migrant bird, singing
an old refrain here and there
my truant gradeschool bike rides
the Kansas sun-warm'd
sunflower-lined blacktop
and the bird makes up its song along the delta.
River like an ever widening crack in the universe.

Gospel thoughts gathered
like plantation cotton.

MADONNA'S "LOVE LIKE A VIRGIN"
(in the manner of Arnaut)

Some will say "appalling"
to "Love Like a Virgin" (a true simile)
a bra falling
No shy peeress in white lace, she.

All classes meet
in her song of love
the woman of the street
turns swoon of royal dove
to roll, to rub the stage
of delight and desire
the ballerina's paraphrase
lips, hips and sexual fire.

Great challenge and threat
to all pretentious fools
worker, professional, bureaucrat,
who lose their tools
when facing this talent
that sulks and erupts
to such embellishment
the strut bust lusts.

The poppies turning
black as witches.
Their scarred greying faces
like hip hag muppets
in red and white crepe.
Pink flames from white
blood turned brown.

WAS POE AFRAID?
(Read with Huncke and Bremser at The Cross St. Bar)

On these same brick streets of
Baltimore tonight—was Poe afraid?

Afraid of the florescent eyes of dogs,
the raven's reflection, the rats scat
through sawdust in Hollins Market,
the smell of rot and burlap thick as fur.

Afraid of roaches, disease, of poverty,
loud poverty boom-box crackle crack whip
poor ponies pulling carts full of greens
up Greene Street—overloaded with greed.

Afraid of the thick sky over foggy tavern door
On Cross Street's cloud-draped rummaged
crimson cloak, threading from the hill
down to the curling dark water bay.

Afraid of statues with iron poet capes flowing
in formal rapture and cast hollow spirit
looking down cold upon those animated
walking and talking past old doorways

Afraid of the wine, the drugs, the vault
of alcoholic shoreline's fractal ragged fault
floating in a dream grave afraid to yell
smug disciples repeating versions of hell.

The whirl of a wash, a tangled thread
sets an alarm that turns to dread
makes the vision flow instead into
creation and how such grace is fed.

Life is a poor host grabbing guests who came
swirling great pleated sheets wrapping the stars
leaving, streaming party coils to their last cars
some on twilight's slightly twisted cane.

LISTENING TO CHARLEY CHRISTIAN
AND THINKING OF HARLEM 1940s

Say, ofay, voices from a
yellow Buick convertible
on a red brick road
loitering against the curb
sunny Sunday afternoon
Be Bop
cool live relaxed
Lucky Strike red wrapper
red apple
and ba-nan-a
back gold glaze
French Gypsy neon
Jam Jam Jam
tapestry session
Pennsylvania Hotel
Black La Salle!

IN PARIS

In Paris the black and red
flags fly from the Sorbonne.
In Paris workers and students unite,
and I look for a precedent of world revolution—
find out Communists
are bourgeois pigs.
General de Gaulle tells the people
that the "shit-in-the-beds" would get 'em—
cut out and left them
in a political vacuum
until they burned their own cars
and cried for a leader.
His experience and southern C.R.S.
superior to the
sling-shots of cerebral students.

Charges begin at two a.m.
The delicate shops intact
by noon the stones
are in place in the street
the cars hauled off,
gas in the air, the Frenchman has his lunch.
If you want to miss the revolt
go to bed early and wake up at noon.

Outside the Coupole the sweet
bums are kissing à la Genet.
The active ones anyway . . .
not those grown formless
huddled against the wall,
skin draped, as if
pinched from a rotten soft peach.

And in the Coupole the very rich,
and very young, and very beautiful
boys and girls caught slumming
talk all night of how they wreck

their cars and how many speeding
tickets they have, and properly
surrounded by their entourage
they buy their stage and leave.

A newspaper reads "BYE, BYE, BOBBY"
and all about gun-crazed America.
Late that night the cafe is cleared
with police and tear gas outside.
Stranded with the journalist,
I take a napkin,
wrapped it around my face
and camp, "Can you imagine
an American
in this situation without a gun?"

And then one evening before the
delicate French moon trailed
above the balconies of filigree
dripping pools of silver and sky through
black shadowed trees
Pam walked on bricks
of childhood streets.

The next day we lit a candle for Kennedy
in Notre Dame in front
of a statue with a serpent at its feet.

SONG OF THE BOWERY 1969
from the opera singer's window

Throw down the key my sweet
get me off this fuckin' street
On stairs to artists' lofts bums sleep
like ghosts from razed burlesque halls
Of ancient poolrooms and eight balls
of faded wreaths, pennants, and the play
Long since blended in dismal golden gray.

Throw down the key and let me in.
I gotta new felt tip pen and want
to write about vicarious pimp sins
and old opium dens off Mott St.
I wanna buy in! Like they say in old
Hell's kitchen... factory loft now filled
with opera scores and magazines.

The song begins like tapes going round in my brain
pimps, poets, presidents, piss, dogshit and trains
nothing happening, no parts fit, the same at the top
as at the bottom, the tape goes around
one side loses, the other gains
the space in the middle remains the same.

You walk past me, I walk past you
and the bums walk crazily
from side to side fighting the gravity of puke
beneath the seagull's liberty.
Throw down the key, my sweet
and get me off this street.
The pimps are dressed in white.
Suburbanites drive pimp Cadillacs too
shop at stores full of lamps and La Machines
slam car doors to lock them into
the American dream and Wall St. rates.
Bend down and kiss the asphalt.

You voted for it, rip it off . . . scheme . . .
make your play in the losing street scene.

Turn away from the young street gun quickly,
a subterranean rose drama in Little Italy.

(Rosetta with your dreamy eyes
lips grown calm at fourteen
half smile, half scowl no one knows).

Switchbladed from love to hate
slick as the pockets of your
black motorcycle jacket.

A replay of Dallas on T. V.
Throw down the key.
Who knows but what super star
may fall out of the American orbit tonite.

Hey man, there's Van Gogh
ringing the bell on Amsterdam.
A thousand merchants bathetically
meeting his eyes. He lends an ear.

Past Bill Burroughs' bunker
the ancient Y, I know, and I have
to say good day to John Giorno.
Scat past Andy's Factory
for fifteen minutes in the future.
To Max's K.C. speedshift
the night is fluid and swift
red and white surrealistic gate
end of Lexington Avenue.

Fear and crime
kaleidoscopic dada vu
cut out my face
put in you.

Gladiator rock bite
superbike 2,000cc
recurring odysseys
collage of purple night
and brown cafes.
Let it all hang out
put it all back in
and the cockroaches shall inherit
the grime, the pills, the alcohol,
the overdose of life and the spit
that the bums sizzle in barrel fires
burning on the Bowery...rubbing hands
they play the block jive of broken banjos
the last tangos with old Marlon Brandos.
When the cold nor'easter throws her cruel net
over the waterfront, they'll all be dead
from trying to reach her great love
while we all drag our fucking patriotic wings
past the locked cars and windows of new lamps
to praise and bend down to kiss the asphalt.

June, 1968

CUP OF JOE

Do you know
Truck Stop Joe
Dropped his load
in K.C.M.O.

Oh Oh
Truck Stop Joe
Longs for his boat
In Sausalito

Truck Stop Joe
Twitches across America
In the back of a truck
When he gets to California
He really wants to

Find a girl
Who wants to go

They just show him their bellies
And read the Tarot

BUFFALO BEBOP BLUES
for Richard Houff

Going back to Wichita and rebop the bebop blues
      yes, yes
Going back to Wichitown? And bebop the rebop blues.

Oh your head's too instant
   and your Jell-O mold won't mix,
Your head's too empty
   ain't nothin you can fix.

So I'm going back to Wichita and rebop the bebop blues.
My clutch is slipping but I'll arrive on time
      Oh yes
My clutch went out beside the plastic diner sign
so I'll flag my breaker buddy* out on
      the Interstate line.
I don't use my thumb like a beaver or a buffalo
      no, no
I don't use it like I should no more.

My gear is grinding like it know where to go
 going back to Wichita and bebop the rebop blues.

My gears so worn, I don't even need to shift
     for sure
They may be worn now baby,
      but you still can't catch my rift.

Ain't pullin' no weight baby,
      so I don't need no lows
carrying nothin so I don't need a low
all I need is high and I know how to go
back to Wichititty and bebop around the flo'.

CB lingo
CB lingo for female/male hitchhikers

SANTA CRUZ
For Anne Sex Goddess, Neal's lover

I know how you feel like a woman uncovered,
Slightly wild, beneath the full moon;
I feel the blush of pastured rose.

I feel the passive moon tonight,
and I am not ashamed,
I want to have love made me,
or to get screwed.

I know the moment of young flesh,
Like the kids turning on to fire down the beach,
To be wet with screw,
To be made love to, till shadows ignite each.

Oh! Yes tonight I must build a boardwalk
across the Pacific, with red shoes and carnivals on.
Yes tonight while the moon lights Point Sur.

I want a free-for-all where ragtime cells
soar mad with moonbeam skaters,
Decoding wave and spark and seas,
and energies hang down from pine and star,
fresh, sweet, like Kid Cupid's slim ovaries.

DECEMBER
(Wichita, Kans.)

Awkward, standing near soiled anklets of death,
money in congress for personal rain of arrows,
shot into the eye of pyramids and shackled birds
and white tailed deer cradled in a jet stream.

Guilty as homemade sin. Old Injun. Ugh! Why me?
Here again? C'mon baby, let's run down to the
river. Let your boobie relays just glide past
the sparks of hellish millions that can't buy,

place we gathered ferns in lighter years
tickling the blood veins of your temples
somewhere in Kansas through the stars to
difficulty. By wandering trees stripped cold.

Mother old and stooped in the kitchen
at 5 a.m, preparing for work. Her old
tough pioneer hands explaining coils
assembled at her minimum wage job.

She who plowed with the John Deere tractor
when I was a babe in a wooden box on its
floorboard, watching the huge tires pull
across the prairie. Smelling fresh earth

turning in sudden spell of wonder. Unconscious
king of renewal opened for the wheat seed.
The pop pop of the two cylinders pinging
into the magnetic singing of space.

High to the poles of earth where birds fly out.
Messengers from the inner sun. Who will pray
in the silent vertigo of light and speed?
Who can gaze into trees without seeing a pattern?

She, now, grievous, worried, shaking her head
. . . as a swimmer tossing water from his hair.
Worried about my alcoholic sister, in jail,
or somewhere in Mission Dist., San Francisco.

A rough bar, perhaps, on Valencia St.
where broken Indians fight vague battles.
Her thoughts lost in worry like her
car keys. "Now where did I put them?"

Jehovah's Witness at the door. Pentecost
on telephone. Billy Graham on the radio.
"Who," as they say in gambling circles,
"really has the nuts on the tables?"

Christmas conjoined on the personality
cross, stuck in the mystic kingdom of self.
The streets swell in holiday bulbs inside
a floating world of bubbles and goods.

A carnival of alchemy in the snow
early frost stigmata on the hay.
Roots in the center of black earth
where Indians begged for food.

. . . Passed my old house remembering
impossible dances out the door
onto the grass holding pages of
wild poetry I could not understand.

Beautiful and tragic wing of youth.
And now a hollow feeling, north,
like winter white water. A rendezvous in inner
space. Mike says home is where the hurt is.

There then? Would go east again to
spring blue wood, or south to red
summer fire. Or complete the cross
west again to autumn yellow gold.

APRIL 5, 1997
for James Stauffer

Chirp, chirp, chirp
Ginzy gone
I broadcast the seeds
bread crumbs from the compost
for little animals and birds

Chirp on the phone, chirp on the radio
broadcasting them seeds
Janine left a message on the phone
I read it in chirp cyberspace

Up Lancaster St. we drove
past the bank on East Hill Road
New house where'd you come from
another house along this road

that one didn't used to be there
yet another on the way to the farm
that was the idea of a farm for poets, etc.

The great view of the Mohawk Valley
its early spring mauves and browns
old crops of gold fields stalks

Didn't take the shortcut where
Ray froze his fingers round a beer can
walking to Cherry Valley in a blizzard

Turn off the paved road
Bad hill bad ruts from spring washes
Peter needs to get that tractor
and haul some dirt and gravel

Like he usta with the manure spreader
Julius faithfully standing on the hitch
Big tractor at the corner
have to walk in here
Roads all wet, parts covered with snow

Hear the birds already
Get the bread pieces
throw a few
tie my shoe

Walk down the slushy ruts
through mud and snow
old craggily cherry tree
must be a hundred

You said the old ones were wiser
"broadcast" the bread a metaphor
when you were born, tho most had radio
more bread for the bashful birds

Stop here to rest and share
my hard bagel with the birds
hmm. That doesn't taste bad
maybe I'll eat it meself.

Hardly a sound up here in hushed forest
the snow is silent in the deer tracks
Pam says the daffodils are in bloom

I'll put some bread crumbs on the porch
not on this chair with peeling paint
Bread on the old maple tree
bread on the rock for innocent creatures

A rag is hanging on the old clothesline
and the barn door needs repair
the whole barn actually, I'll leave
some crumbs by the outhouse and
the barn and the cherry tree
On the road back a woodpecker
breaks the silence, hammering perfectly
like a Whitman carpenter
Burdock sticks like Velcro
Bread on the windowsill

bread on the rock
Old truck rusting away
new tires rotted in place
never helped anyone
get anywhere or nowhere anymore.

The air always changes on East Hill
like the atmosphere of heavens
the stars come down to
a respectable level in
case you need to chat with 'em

It is heavy now and the sun is
burning like chrome in the grey sky
the woods are mauve and brown dark green
the green and grey neglected cottage
weathers by the green and grey pound

The mountains and the sky are all blue
various shades enshrouding the Evergreens
white birch arises from moss green rock
of old hills and forests

You walked me to the boundary
twenty-nine years ago
probably talking of Whitman and Death
Now you know

In Beat style, written for the occasion, never edited.

SONG FOR NEAL CASSADY

for John Cassady

Oh really really Neal
his first love was the automobile

Drove a '34 Ford with suicide doors
    and stick shift on the floor
    Draggin' down main to Colfax Avenue

Jumpin' in the back seat boulevard
    kicked back watching asses in the rearview
    cruising past the high school

Clock on the dash reading 10:18
past the neon diner
    last stop for Benzedrine
    and onward to another scene

Chicks would rob a joint
    just to buy him food

One hand on the wheel
    the other in her mood

The blue-eyed kid and the wild-eyed bobby soxer
    California surfers Tarot card sharks and word shooters

Found Ann-Marie in Frisco like a hurricane cock
    didn't need the Sexual Freedom League

Driving with white pills and pot
    but was really addicted to the wheel

Came back to Old San Francisco
    Flower children all over the streets

Carried star struck Ann-Marie in his arms
    the Denver Kid he never returns

Traded her Chevrolet coupé
    for an old Pontiac

Up the hills, down the curves
    gear it down, pump the brakes
Old mother Ginsberg's back seat drivin'
    turning toward the Avalon drinking a couple of liters
    walking   down Van Ness
    jumping parking meters

One hand on the gearshift
    the other copping a feel

One hand up her dress
    the other on the wheel

Stole a car in Denver just to hear it peel
    just like drivin' in the races
Stole a car in Denver just to hear it squeal

He moved so fast
    he had one foot in Cincinnati the other in Kalamazoo

Women knew just what to do
    and all wanted him to be true

Parked in front of Gough Street
    in a 50's red and white Plymouth Fury

Just back from seeing Kerouac, in a hurry
    patrol car in the mirror
    the old white and blacks

Drove past someone with some little white pills
    heading into town

He jumped in the driver's seat
    and spun that Fury around.

The roads were paved with powder all the way to Mexico
    and train tracks shined in the moon
First Road Warrior
    what he did wrong, he never knew

NOVEMBER 3, 1998 DARK AFTERNOON

November, Bremser,
and the clouds are heavy metal
rolling oe'r the vacant brick of Utica
where Ray lies in his death throes
at the Faxton Cancer Hospital.

It's not a happy sight, a
finality about the rooms and service
his roommate's exposed privates
both he and Ray seem far away.

In and out of sensed reality
I fear to say, eyes like animals in cages
Ray's eyes sometimes intense
screaming "I want to die"
not in a philosophical mode
but the growl used for prison guards
rattling his bones against the
iron bars of New Jersey.

Squirts of daylight on the sidewalk
like used rubber gloves thrown
among the slimy Autumn leaves
Study the sight, oh latter night Beats.

Another is passing into the night
like TV. tonight Jimmy Smit
on NYPD the line of fictive reality
unto death, what to do with life's purpose?
If it's to understand life (loved the old comedies)
from those eyes just make ourselves over
Ray watch the old realities in black and white
He pulls on the bed rails : "I want to die."
His eyebrows move and he briefly conducts
a conversation he can't partake in
or a Katchaturian concert or a poem.
He leans back, eyes glazed, goes elsewhere
further than shooting up decades ago

the history gone like our rides for Terpin hydrate
finding village drugstores while the world went on.

What history can a human have. The history gone
the religions, the politics, the last fiction...not that
Faith, miracles, and belief isn't real
there's just never enough to go around.

Don't tell me his spirit has to hitch a ride
'round about midnight'
to make a visitation when the sky
rolled back its spheres to let the gold sun
wail like a sax over the stage of East Hill
for an original hipbeatster camping at
the Committee on Poetry farm
where he said he used to talk more shit
than the radio which he didn't own.

APOCALYPSE ROSE
San Francisco, Tenderloin, 1963

The Juke-box begins its song:
futuristic mirage blossoms
dimensions of accelerated fortune tellers
Leaving his coffee,
the boy from nowhere
dials any combination of numbers
on the telephone,
smiles under the beat
of NOWHERE TO HIDE.
The night that shades his darkened eyes
unwinds into mistaken paradise.
Numbed with gravity
the song grows fainter.
Those closer to the earth
are last to go.
Image passed on streets long vacant.

*   *   *   *

The hand that strikes the match at night
soon may grasp the torch of liberty.
While a dog tail dipped into a wound
holds the mirror union of the senses.

And all in war of space and time,
I dream to drink with you
from the fountain of strength, and wait
for an unbelievable date to the movies.

Or isn't there a job for you in space
Catherine, with your metal sandwich?
Let's keep the conversation hermetic,
for soon even midnight will be plastic.

I will forget the ads I read
in this Mechanix Illustrated:
"Be a locksmith" and fumble lost keys

of Paradise. I have my own shop now.
Ah, to the movies, where your hero in
black sulphur spurs dives in a wedding of mustangs.
(An eagle collects doorknobs in the afternoon,
the code: In Honor of Autumn.)

*   *   *   *

Do those who cannot see, love darkness?
Does nightingale trade its song for fame?
Are you in human form, calm once more
With your imploding love to blame?

Would you run among sweet wild flowers
To warn of Autumn in ominous tone?
I ask the generation with a hardening smile
If killing goes will love be all alone?

*   *   *   *

If destiny could be bought for latest kicks
Could I sell a man screaming in an hourglass?
Could I sell my pin-up queen for charity?
Tell me, my burning rose, about all this.
Tell me in words I cannot understand,
Because if I do, I will cry to hear
Myself above all others,
And crush you in a fabulous evening.
Then go to my room and rinse my hair in
Cream rinse and think of pill-day Cadillacs
With continental spares and chrome rear ends,
Undercoatings of violet lace.

And read Kustom Kar magazines far into the night . . .
Dreams of billfolds full of money,
Nightmares of conspiracies.
Is this the head I'm stuck with
Born to an age which makes me thirty?

*   *   *   *

Or I may see a laborer in the sun
Who dreamed he was a poet
And wandered over a hill to a shining city
There he peeks into the final version of himself.
And remembers the love songs of warm-bosomed singers
As in the days of dying and rebirth,
Melting in a wilderness of armor
Trembling in fear when the doors flew open.
When poet ran around the globe
Collecting love and rage and tongue,
Anointed with hair oil
Infiltrating the last detail of the universe
. . . Gold coins pouring down the street.
(Before you ran up your hill in ecstasy,
Removed from ghettoes of clamoring style)
. . . asleep in dawn tail fissures
The boy dreams of nights in K. C.
Jr. gangsters, jazz, and Mr. B. Collars,
Chuck Berry, Bill Haley, and Elvis singing.

*   *   *   *

I'm over here, of course,
melting in war stories,
playing a sweet mournful tune
on a hollow flute made from
the bones of dead junkies.
I'm singing the Great Speckle Bird
under the street lights in N.Y.C.
Now I am here, staring out a window,
people moving about
trying to tell each other something,
put your raincoat on do you want to go next
how long since I saw you
and got that old feeling?
I can hear Chet Baker singing,
I get along without you very
well, except when leaves . . .
Yeah, that's total recall.
Can we go somewhere and talk
through the aether?

Remember, the shack on North Main,
night in Dec., soft rain and fog.
I had death throes in my hands
and every road of life closed down.
And you trying to help me
and not go under yourself.
Sick lightning in a far off storm.
Followed the road of those before me to
the West. (Harlow with your name in silk.)

*   *   *   *

Tonight I ride in the
beautiful mountains
in a ragged chartreuse Ford,
under the moon with heaven close
to earth of winding road and sounds of
cymbals and chants and songs like
Wildflower and Moon Over Alabama.
Julio chuckling privately
at moo cows in the pasture,
moon on the dashboard
like a flower . . .
Creator, Destroyer, Preserver.

*   *   *   *

Do not tell the stars
I sing like a traitor
From radio Apocalypse Rose.
Is there something I can say to you
O Radar Queen in Compton's Cafeteria,
Before the puke and blood melt in the street?
Is there a glitter of dragon flame
Through the gold of skid row?
Is there a promise in the bedrooms
Below fixed bayonets of Paradise?
We are linked by our tongues' wall
With hand grenades on our mouths.
There were you before a protest was needed ?

* * * *

Could I walk out the door and say,
"Baby I'm gonna get mine."
But without missing too many meals
I can buy a Polaroid for $29.98,
And take pictures of troops and pickets.
Or Mr. Hyde of Cut Corner who wishes his
was black leather. Or 19 yr. old David,
who burned himself,
left a note reading, Buddhist Monk,
Inquire at Fairoaks St . . .
"I die for all mysterious things."
Or the blind on Market Street
Or the man with no legs,
Perhaps no nearer to panorama than thou.

* * * *

Would you be cruel
if you spent a life
carrying Venus to Mars
with a light in your head?
While under the bridge of forgotten gold,
Betty throws a wine bottle against the wall.
And a wino was stacked in a bed of cardboards
dead for many months smelling.
More cardboards were piled on him
And more winos slept on top of him,
for many months smelling.
When the police dug him out, they said
"He was crushed like a rose in a Bible."

* * * *

Sometimes flowers bloom in spring
unaware of what the summers bring

From now on
today is the most beautiful,

planters have struck against the ground,
grain is overheard on the melon side of night.
The rose has fainted in the mirror.

Where else can Autumn be?
"I'm over here."
Again? . . .
But the windmills chopped the sky.
Are you still there

with spying creators pinned to streetlights?
Turned on too soon to clairvoyant blue?

*   *   *   *

Break the mind trap in time stigmata.
Call back the runaway climax from the
speed of Christmas squared. Because
you seem to know too much just beyond
the conversation. So let's walk down
Market St, where your outline changes
in the mercury of your flaming youth
under marquees on the meat block
where teenage hustlers cruise.

We walk past an old newsreel of Dillinger.
"He smiles on the right side of his face,"
you say, "like Bogart."

Your voice in the fog
lights on the street.

*   *   *   *

The rose that summer held and gave again,
Has grown your form in reappearing dew,
Preserved the fragrance of that time began
When seeds were drops of love in rose-red hue.
But sweet life must nourish on such sorrow,
As each dying makes some men blossom through
The blood that fell on each new tomorrow

And you saw this as I was watching you.
Under the influence of all your stars,
In mirrors of your galaxies of blue,
The hero and his love became your scars
But this rose picked could not be picked anew.
  To measure you and me in full disguise
  I lay beside our rose of paradise.

POSTSCRIPT

... This is Charley, swinging. The time is spring-summer, this year, 1963. The place, Wichita, Kansas, where the golden wheat has just been harvested and the trees are bursting greenery touching tips over the center of the streets. Charley stands in a combination teenage twist and gay bar done up in coral walls lined with gilded store window manikins. He stands at the front of the dance floor before a juke box that has a waterfall behind it and light flowing down its sides, so that he appears to be coming from a neon grotto. His hair is falling over his forehead in a mass of curls, he is wearing dark glasses, a blue-and-silver sport shirt, a metallic gold tie, black tight pants slung low on his hips, and black-and-white saddle oxfords. One hip is slung outward. Up go the hands in the air.

"TWIST!" Shouts Charley.

Up his back runs a ripple like a snake moving, fast. His hips are inscribing a frenzied half-circle in the air. His head bounces and bobbles with jazz-drummer ecstasy. His arms flail, he's almost flying but his feet are planted in the floor, sucking up great electrical currents of earth vibrations.

"It's the vortex!" He shouts. "Can't you feel the forces! Pulling you in! It's twisting in twister land!"

Across the floor toward him dances his blonde college-girl goddess, and she's out of her mad gold pony-tailed head. She's all Charley could dream of exploding into, she's Miss Freeswinging Kansas, Caucasian aflame, descendant of hot-blooded fairy-tale princesses, she moves with classic American grace, she's poised and pure and fashion-hip, she has round arms of love, ready to grab, she won't be brought down, and above the rock and roll, sweet cello strings play for all eternity in that gold head of hers.

They're back at the table where a crowd of us are sitting. They're arm in arm, together again, and I turn on to their beauty aglow with sex.

"This is where it all comes from!" Shouts Charley. "Can't you feel the vibrations? Man, there is so much energy here that you just get near it and flooom! It's got you and swinging you someplace else."

This is Charley's hometown, the land that produced him, and he's back to turn everyone on and get recharged. Everywhere he goes crowds of youth follow him, turning *him* on. Now the brown-limbed teenagers in cutoff jeans and bouffant hair have taken the floor. Their bodies are strong, sunbeautied, and swimming-pool clean, they're eager-high on beer. They are dancing dances they all know, no one touching, boys with girls, girls with girls, boys with boys. All the steps are perfect and harmonious. They are all oh God so beautiful and I know we cannot lose, beyond all certitude of mind mankind will take the stars and crush time with these golden kids, born of our bodies and spirit.

Here Charley is big, here with youth. He is vibrant with sex that knows no separation from love, and hope for and beware of the day its dancing force is turned on you, my friend. Crowds follow him, he is alive with scheme and dream, and he will make it happen *now*. Are you ready? He will, like the morning glory but more aware, unfold himself in the sunburst of today.

Crowds follow him, turned on. He's having a show of his collages at a weird place, the New Mission Care, in the skidrow-trainstation section of Wichita. Charley aggrandizing making bright the legend. Is it a game? How much is glory and how much is morning glory? (He quotes Cocteau: "All art is a card trick.") He has made the Wichita scene happen: bright-eyed campus beauties, long-haired students, careful college professors, waiting-in-limbo artists, shimmy-shake drag queens, long ago pillhead buddies, strange inhabitants of the outposts of Beatsville—all come to soak up Charley energy, to be angered, to be inspired, to lift him up or put him down, but always to be stirred.

Glenn Todd
San Francisco, 1997

FICTION

Neal Cassady, Charles Plymell, outside
1403 Gough Street pad, 1963. Plymell sits
on the first Honda import.

A FABLE:

THE PRINCE OF TIDES

The King of the most powerful land was preparing his reign of peace, freedom, and equality for all his people. The Queen was preparing for birth of the new Prince. But there were problems. His armies were engaged in a conflict they could not win. The young did not want to fight the unknown enemies that the old had made to keep power. Much to the Queen's dismay, who was busy rearing the new Prince, the King had also fallen under the spell of the Sex Goddess who ruled in the Make Believe World.

In order to draw attention from his problems, he promised his people and the Goddess something impossible. The Moon was inviolate and pure through all the millenniums. It was the symbol of an untouched heavenly body. On a hot July day when the seas of the earth were hazy his spacemen set foot on the moon and played a sport. For beings from Earth, landing on the moon was the greatest of all feats, but other Heavenly Bodies grew angry and sent a tremor through space.

The others ordered the moon to multiply the earth beings until they poisoned themselves with their sciences, inventions, and technologies that they thought would better their race and protect themselves. The toxins made them act strangely and kill each other in inhuman and unpredictable ways. The other Heavenly Bodies also put a curse on the Sex Goddess who died mysteriously, reportedly taking her own life. The King was assassinated, his brain stolen, and the event so obscured that the Queen and her people would never know the truth. The toddler Prince saluted his father's horse-drawn casket. The King's brother was also assassinated and tragedy befell more of the family.

The Prince grew into the handsomest and most desired by all peoples. Even a Princess from another country came to visit him. The millennium was drawing to a close. Strange events happened more frequent. The Princess' great beauty was crushed by a new lifestyle of high-speed technology and metal. With his wife and her sister by his side, the Prince flew his new sleek-wing'd technology into a July haze just a few years after the Queen had died. Before the new millennium, in the same month the King had made the moon his conquest, fabulous remains washed ashore in silent pieces where the Queen had once played with the child Prince while the King governed his people.

THE SMELL OF LIGHTNING

In the old septic mountains of New York, lived Dangerous Dan, car guru, subsisting on beer, Camels and pot. He played drums, and lived in Cockroaches' building. He always had some esoteric part from a bike or other vehicles around his pad. He grew up reading S. Clay Wilson's pirates. With his flintlock pistol, he shot a hole through the wall. The "Troopers" came and took his gun. The Troopers were a big thing in small villages...like an extended family. The locals acted like guilty children around them. Welfare families used Troopers for their father figures.

To Dan, the thought of eating was a disorder. He played his drums for Misty and kept her car running. She was his symbolic chick, names changed or evolved. Like the old song, "I was in love with you baby before I could call your name." Misty had gotten to know some of the back-to-earth women who stood in their gingerbread kitchens all winter making bread, talking about food and sex emotional armor like hard elm tree. They wore hiking boots and liked to do men things. When they kissed you, they stuck their butts out so there won't be any touching in the genital area."

Dangerous Dan complained of not sleeping well due to the quietness of the nights. He had been used to the noise of Manhattan and was suffering his Postcharismatic Blues Syndrome. As he slept, he saw what appeared to be a giant fountain of antimatter emptied outward at a distance so far only its pulse was left. Charley picked up on it.

The first fallen snow was one of the most poetic of the season's rituals. Misty looked sweetly at Charley and said, "You say you will believe in something...yes, there has to be something. The eons are empty without something...the stars cannot be stuck to the black sky without some kind of glue."

" I want to glue you to me like a milky way of smeared semen."

"Tell me, and I will wait to hear your voice—and wait to see; tell me you want me, and I will alert old Arsenic Angels Wind."

Charley moved closer.

"Do you want to see my organ?"

"No," I mean this.

Misty pulled out the little accordion montage she had made.

"Oh, Misty, I will always believe in your greatness."

She did not let his hands continue.

"What is it with this generation. Don't they know it's their history? Their time? Well fuck you Misty Moo Moo. I'm a loser, too. Used to jack off to you, broke, in the toilets in Reno, Nevada, when I thought you were Lady Luck . And yet, we know that when it comes to Love, we have to learn the lesson over and over again. As fucking simple as Heartbreak Hotel. I think cloning is the only way out. Clone it all. Why not? All our lives are spent wanting to be something we're not, watch our imagined imaged on the tube, wanting what we can have. Clone it and fulfill all those mad desires. Desire is poverty, and I'm tired of poverty. Noise is poverty, too.

Noisy desires. A desire stadium full of mad hype and universal flame. I want peace! Tesla said that was the wish of everyone and that his electric current would annihilate space. And I say, "Don't time warp me baby if you want to stay where you are. Everything is ambiguous, even your symbolism, but at least the big fat Buddha doesn't torture me so. You won't even show me your pussy. I don't have time for this shit! I have to tighten the doors and windows, put plastic on the to help stop the shit-winter cold. But I guess it's better to live in Shitsville than have civilization bust down your metal door, and barricade your children in the diesel smoke."

The next morning was sunny. The wind blew through the late fall-dried cornstalks rustling like the sounds of buried seas, and suddenly a spangled pheasant flew from the road. Charley got up and shoveled the walk. As he cleared a spot, a huge mound of snow slid from the roof and covered it again.

"I have to get a tire fixed this morning," said Charley. "I'll have to drive 28 miles to the garage. Nothing open here.

He was joined by Fuzzy who helped take the tire to a larger town.

"We can fix the tire; it needs a Vulcan patch. But our machine doesn't work. Needs a new wire."

"Do you have any used tires you can put on the rim?"

"Well, let me see wha' size it is."

The mechanic took off his gloves and brushed away the dirt from the side of the tire. One of the men standing there said it looked like a 6.00 x 14. This started a round of speculation, you go by the number on the tire, which always seems to be obscure and ambiguous until the man looks in a catalog to change the equation of the whole thing, and you realize there must be reasons for this somewhere, or is it built into something, some overriding plan to keep the economy growing?

"I know some guy down the street might ha' some old tires."

Charley turned to the mechanic. "Can you give us a lift down the street, ya think?"

"Well, I wd. Bu I 'ave this one jab to gi out and I'm wa-in for my ba-er-i to charge. The big charge is broke so I 'ave to plub it in. It takes a few hours."

The sun will be going down shortly and the cold will begin to set in, Charley thought as he noticed they were talking funny. One started grinning a cold smile as his eyes focused like a hunter or trapper ready for his game. His lips were white and curved inward; his teeth rotted and his sneakers full of holes.

"Maybe it's the voltage regulator," said Fuzzy, wanting to sound mechanical.

"I don't think so," replied the mechanic. "I checked tha- and the ba-er-i cables. It always star-ed righ' up all win-er, never had no prob'ms before. Bea' me."

"That's OK, we can walk," said Charley as he began rolling the tire through the slush and snow.

"Y'know, it sounds funny the way they don't say their T's, the O's are sometimes pronounced A," Fuzzy whispered.

Well, there's a reason for it," said Charley. "This is dairy country and there's a lot of milk around here. Now, milk's OK for most people in normal amounts, but it makes some others deteriorate, the ear is especially vulnerable. There're a lot of poor people spend all their foodstamps for junk food and then think they can make it up with milk, so they drink gallons of it a day. Among other effects, it makes your jaw loose. The muscles in the jawbone become weak 'cause you're not sucking or chewing, only drinking, and there is not enough exercise to keep out harmful muscle deterioration. When the jaw becomes lax in cold climates, it's hard to say the T's before the next word because too much cold gets in. This gets fixed in the language. It's a diet problem, really."

"Let me roll it a while, Charley." Fuzzy rolled the tire as it wobbled relentlessly from side to side like a wild drunken person.

"Aw, shit."

"What's the matter?"

"I just rolled it through dog shit."

The snow and slush had turned brown and Fuzzy got it on his hands. He went back to the garage where everyone was unwrapping chocolate bars.

"Where's the bathroom?"

"Ba' there," one grinned.

Fuzzy walked the length of the building which was filled with cars and tractors taken apart to be fixed.

"It don' wark though!" Yelled someone as Harry was about to enter. "The pipes froze las' night and they's no water, so you can' flush."

Fuzzy came back and picked up some snow to wash his hands. One of the farmers went over to the candy machine and deposited a coin. Gadgetry was their connection to the outside world of commerce and invention. The candy bar didn't come out. He pounded on the machine. Finally he got the owner to open the machine. As Charley and Fuzzy left, there was a heavy smell of manure, fresh chocolate, and old grease. The men lined up, their lips parted in a half smile making a taut pale ring around their mouths, a tight milky rind of flesh hollowed in their reddened cheeks. Their hands were strong and big as catchers' mitts as they lifted the door in a better position to stop the wind. The sign "Fud's Garage" dangled from the door.

"There's quite a chill factor out there," Charley said.

"I'll git the door," one said.

Charley and Fuzzy went to get Dangerous Dan.

"Dangerous Dan, we need your help."

"Cool, man."

Dangerous Dan looked at the tire with curiosity, as if it would open up a whole set of decisions, motivations, and movements for the next few days or weeks.

"Hmmmm, he said, "actually I might find a tire to replace it." The cryptic markings on the side of the tire set off another round of speculation.

"We have to get up to Ben's place. Can we borrow your V.W.?"

"It's cool, I guess. I'm having a little problem with the battery or the starter, I don't know which."

The temperature was dropping rapidly and it had barely been above freezing all day. The car was stuck. Fuzzy and Charley lifted up on the bumper and the back fender.

Charley fell down. "Holy shit!"

"Yeah, the fender came off."

Charley stood holding a section of fender that had been eaten away by rust and salt. Dangerous Dan took it in his hands and studied it.

"Hmmm," he said as he threw it over the cliff into the dark. "Has anyone got an extra pair of gloves? This rim is bent. I had to swerve off the road so I wouldn't hit some dogs that ran in front of me. I must've hit a rock and bent the rim." He got the jack out and put it on the icy driveway. "I don't see a jack stand, man. Do you see one?" Something about Dangerous Dan liked the challenge. He liked jacking his car up without a stand and the jack slipping on the ice just missing him. He tried over and over and finally got the tire on. As they smoked another joint, he began coughing violently and shaking.

"You'd better take care of that cough," Charley said, taking the weed from Dangerous Dan's index finger and thumb with his own.

"Yeah, I know, I went to the doctor. He said I might have hepatitis or the flu. It's probably the flu. There's a flu bug going around." His nose dripped onto his gloves.

Fuzzy felt a shiver in his chest as he stamped his feet trying to keep warm. The wheels spun back and forth on a frozen patch. Finally they reached a dry patch and jumped in the car and waved. They picked up Misty on the way.

They arrived at Ben's farmstead. White centuries-old gravestones tilted out of the ground. Fuzzy began walking and cursing faster, trying not to think, but stumbling ahead in the dark, lost; yet proceeding somehow to a familiar place. The images of the early homesteaders flashed in his mind— hacking out a living, surviving against the rough winters; he noticed that the due dates on the old gravestones were the winter months. He pictured the craggy oak drawn down on the bobsled to keep the fire going...the best maple syrup brought to town down the road past the giant hemlock. A pure scene, never to be seen again except in paintings. In some future mansion our little scene won't hang, thought Fuzzy as he looked into the evening. Haze seeped through the clouds and rolled over the new snow, turning the landscape blue as though blueing in the wash had spilled over the white sheets. The colors had whitened like a reverse photograph. A bright day-glo orange and a brush of purple finished the narrow lines of sunset.

They went inside. Ice had formed on the inside of the windows. The old horsehair plaster had crumbled and cracked in a few spots; each layer of torn wallpaper revealed a new dream, a new generation, a new style, like a graph of the ages, it had peeled back, layer from layer.

"Damn! It's cold in here!"

"Let's get a fire burning!"

A woodbox for dry kindling was always kept full in the pantry room for survival needs. They hurried to the box and lifted the lid.

"Empty!" Charley yelled.

"Empty? What the hell do you mean?"

"I mean there ain't nuthin' but a note here on this pizza box. 'Ben, we couldn't find anymore dry wood-had to leave, but will be back and gather some soon. Be cool. Love, Limpy, Moe & the musical sleeping bag twins.' Those goddam Hippies! Those patch-assed creeps. Yuppie retreads!"

"What'll we do now?" Asked Fuzzy, trying to calm Charley down.

"We've been shit upon, again, a generation of losers; they don't know what it takes to get along in this fucking world. They all come from instant comfort, and they never think of anyone else. All they do is take, just take—that's all—take—they never give. They never add, never build, never want to do anymore than what's needed. That's just like them not replacing the wood. They could have gotten some from under the snow and put it inside to dry out for the future. That's it. They never prepare for anything. They don't know survival, order, importance, future! What do you think General Washington would do if he had to muster an army again in Harvard Square? They would just look and hiss, 'Who is this fool?' Meanwhile he would have to recruit the busboy at the local motel, the bartender with no teeth. The blacksmith and stable boy."

"Let's build a fire quick! What can we use?"

"Here, out in this backroom, quick. Here's an old captain's chair. Bust it up. It's oak, it'll burn good. And this wall— they're tearing this one down to insulate. We can take some of the lathing."

They began taking off chunks of plaster; the lathing was hand-split and irregular. The cold dust swirled in the room like the breath of a ghost whispering its love after snorting a mummy's cocaine. They started a fire in the woodstove and sat there watching it—fascinated as though it were a new discovery.

"We'd better go out and get some wood to dry near the stove," Fuzzy offered.

"Ah to hell with it. We're not going to be here that long—least possible effort—they should have replaced the wood—no real value—push for whatever can be gotten out of it—it's all symbolized with this empty box—they don't understand the old lessons—use what you need, and if you can, add a little when you replace it—that's the only way out of this world—no instant switch on the infrared magnitude that opens the sky—just a little grace—the wind through the birch sounding like—" Charley faded.

Misty went over and whispered in Charley's ear, "Lets go upstairs to bed, and I'll make you warm."

An invitation to sex from a woman is better than dope. The bed looked inviting; it was wide and had a box around it. The blankets looked warm. Charley reeled over and pulled Misty down on top of him.

"Goddamn-son-of-a-bitch! Help!"

"What's the matter?"

"I think I broke something!"

"Are you OK?" Yelled Fuzzy as he ran up the crude stairway noticing the third step which had pulled away from the nails.

"Are you all right?"

"Yeah, I guess," Charley said, slipping the palms of his hands under his buttocks and shakily levering onto his elbows.

"What the hell is this?"

"It's a waterbed."

"It's frozen solid! It's an icebed! A frozen fuckin' icebed! It's some kind of curse! Help me up.

Let's get the hell out of here."

They got in the car, but it wouldn't start.

"Now what to do?" Cried Misty.

"Don't worry, said Charley, "We can roll to get it started. We can get down to my friend's house even in this white-out.

"Who's your friend?"

"Soddy Slim Moddy. He lives down the road."

"Does he have a waterbed?"

"He may not have that, but he has a phone."

They got in the Bug and bumped and clattered down the hill and around a big curve, came upon a little shack nestled in a forest. White snow obliterated the trail. A gas lamp was burning in the window. They knocked on the door and stamped their shoes.

"Hi guys, what's happening?"

"It's getting cold out there."

"Yeah, c'mon in. I was just fixing up some tea and brown rice. Would you like some?"

"Here, put some soy sauce on it."

"I have to go easy on this. It makes me fart too much."

"Say, could I use your phone?"

"Sure."

Charley picked up the phone...

"ermth ltyal magn nabz"

"Oh, I forgot to tell you. The answering machine froze last night. Just when I was expecting an important message, too.

"It had to do these theories of energy I've been working on."

"The frozen message?"

"Who is this guy?" Misty whispered to Charley when Soddy went to get some wood.

"His real name's Warren Moddy III. A Yale prep school dropout who wants to get cow shit on his shoes and wear torn overalls— likes the flies buzzing round his head— that sort of thing."

"What do the villagers think of him?"

"They wonder why he looks dirt poor. They never heard of dirt rich. They work on the farm all day, which is a dirty job, sure, but then they like to clean up at night and look good in town. Now, here's someone who goes around like dirt poor. He lives filthy, but really, he's rich. Another trust fund idler, brings cheap wine to a party."

A bareness seemed to swoop down upon them like a big hollow icy mouth. The snow turned a brilliant white under the

dark branches which levitated in the breeze like terrible bearded figures in a frozen ballet. The night became a language of
its own, each curve some kind of gesture, each joint, its own
exclamation. A branch entwined in another branch, interracial,
sporadic, broken, a fearful flight from cusp to cusp, horrible
wing branches flopped in the soggy cold underbrush above
them, epileptic branches topped with snow loomed great in
seizure. With craggy skin, the giant elms had stood in great
wisdom and vision; they were pitifully diseased, exposing their
rotted hearts and oozing crotches. No landmarks left except
the road. The hypnotic snow had a mind of its own and could
wrap the mental rule. It could cover all other season's cruel-
ties. Charley recited Emerson's "You shall not be overbold
when you deal with Arctic cold."

"What are you doing, Soddy?" Charley yelled out into the
cold.

"I'm trying to fix this generator."

"Fix this generation?"

"Generator! These generator batteries have run down. I
think it's in the alternator, the lights died down."

"Don't you have electricity?"

"Well, yes, yes and no. I got mine and I got theirs. C'mon
in, I think I'll plug in theirs. Sit down and I'll go to the cellar for
some more potatoes. I've boiled some already. This here's the
potato water, want some? It's good for you."

"No thanks. Do you have any coffee?"

"Hmmm, no. Let's see. I have tea. Sit down. Here!" He
handed Fuzzy a stack of Whole Earth Catalogs to fill in the
caneless chairs.

"Oh, antiques."

"Where's your bathroom, Soddy?"

"It's back there, but you have to go outside."

"Shitter problems?"

"Oh, the ram jet water line goes uphill and it freezes up
sometimes. The sewer line goes uphill, too. What the hell. We
have to boil the water."

"Yeah, better boil the water, been a bug going 'round."

A serious looking woman appeared from the next room. "That's my lady, Mantra Woman," said Soddy. She wore an old fashioned dress and apron over logger's boots and had been baking bread on the wood stove.

"I'm making some bread. You want something to eat?"

"Yeah, tha'd be nice."

She had long dark hair and a nice belly under the apron.

"I hope you like my bread."

"What did you put in it?"

"A little bit of everything," she said, giggling and lighting up a joint.

"Smells good."

"Yes, it' going to be good. I'm putting in some oatmeal and raisins, wheat germ, won't that be good? Nuts and honey and molasses. Mix in some whole wheat flour."

"Wanna hear some Dylan? Mantra Woman just got back."

"From where?"

"Pakistan."

"Wha'd she do there?"

"She begged in the streets."

"Was it fun?"

"I don't know."

Soddy scraped the bottom of a shoe box. "Wanna smoke some Colombian?"

"Smells good," said Charley.

"Sure, why not," said Soddy a bit uncomfortably. "I was going to tell you about this thing I was working on. I have the Defense Department interested in a certain diagram I've formulated. A kind of grid.

"Can you talk about it?"

He began to look like a mixture of Bogart and Don Knotts. His eyes rolled upwards and around the corners as if there was some hidden threat. An invisible spore of paranoia seemed to quicken in his face: the dangerous world surrounded him ready to slap him down again. He looked over his shoulder and put his briefcase on his lap and opened the world map on it. He turned the map upside-down.

"Now here it is, you see the figures emerging on the ocean floor. You see, everything evolves in mythological and anthropological form at the same time with physical history. The characters are like myths. Each myth had a geological parallel. Just like now how our brain waves are at the frequency at which the length of a radio wave equals the circumference of the earth. These things happened and were frozen in history.

"Like Persephone?" Misty tried.

"That's it. You see this one form." He pointed to the southeast ocean ridge. "This is the lower torso of a female figure. As you see, her gown is made up of ridges where other civilizations did something like strip mine for energy. And when the natural forces were upset, the whole upheaval came overnight. Everything went inside itself; reversed itself, if you will. It will do so again."

Soddy adopted an academic tone. "The rape of the planet is not metaphor, I need."

Charley interrupted. "You mean like that ancient Hopi chief with knowledge of the amalgamated Buddha-Aztec-atavistic-swastika? According to their religion, once their sacred geographical circle is penetrated by outside forces it sets up an environmental or ecological chain reaction that cannot be stopped.

"I say no mining for uranium. The change has begun. The Karma of America is clear. The taking from, and abuse of, has to have its returns. It's the implicit law that runs through existence like a simple rerouted creek. Use the effigies! Stop dumping of low level waste. These cause tiny erosions in our giant complex society. But as the subtle erosion becomes small on every level the web is broken. The more complex it becomes, the more subtle the erosions the whole formula changes. Civilization is terror."

"At least, in error, and our dirty genes are tossed back in the wash."

"So, there you have it, after the waste, the mountains of coffee grounds and bones, the plastic filler cracks in a lopsided earth, the ozone violated, the vinyl wedge clogging the resonance, we must change it! The model cannot be seen dancing 50 fathoms deep. Her spine ridge is frozen in dance. The mid-Indian Ocean Ridge. And her arms—her arms are outflung. One goes along the southwest Indian Ocean Ridge. The other reaches under India—the Carlesberg Ridge makes up her neckbone. Then there's something she's handing to the male torso who's body is the mid-Atlantic Ridge. You see it here, his legs on both sides of Greenland. And you see those patterns underneath the oceans. What is it? Do you remember the dance?"

He pointed to the outline of the male dancer on the map. "His ear would be right in the deepest part of the Atlantic Ocean. Right here by the Bermuda Triangle. I guess that's the inner ear. The vortex of the inner ear."

"Vertigo."

"Bingo."

"Ergo, how deep the vertigo. That's when I contact the beings inside the earth who have hidden along the crystal crevices and developed special powers. If you trace the triangles of the vortices, the actual physics of the great balance is where certain lines intersect and become apparent. From Marina Kia to Easter Island, the survivors of ancient civilizations and the modern apocalypse will cross in geographical position. On the same triangle of crystal is the Bermuda Triangle on the Rio Grande Rise, off the coast of Sao Paulo. There is a Triangle under the ocean off Sao Paulo on the other side of Nozca Ridge projectile strip. The intersecting lines of the triangle then go on to Mt. Tabat. Then down to the Mozambique Plateau near where they recently thought there were nuclear blasts. The line off the triangle leads to Mt. Everest down to Cape Inscription near where the Voyager dropped. Whenever the ozone layer is pierced along the alignments there is a combustion. If, of course, the ozone layer is disturbed on a large scale the combustion becomes apocalyptic in proportion."

"But what does that have to do with the Defense Department?"

"Well you see there were cases of spontaneous human combustion at an exact time along the grid which were never reported. The disappearance of personnel. The coincidence would not have been known if I had not been watching at that moment when there was an incident of combustion nearby. I'm not going to tell you what it looked like. I thought I had gone off the deep end, so to speak, for sure. I ran to the telephone and call the Suicide Prevention Center...and..."

"What'd they say?"

"They put me on hold. I finally found this doctor who got a serious response from the Defense Department. They advised me to stay in touch until I got a response from the White House. From there every place I stayed something happened. My last pad caught fire and some of my papers were destroyed. I got in touch with Ben who said I could come and stay here in the mountains. Meanwhile I receive a call every so often from Washington advising me to keep in touch for an 'interview'; I gave them this telephone number."

"The one that froze their message?"

"Yeah...meanwhile I had to find a job or get some kind of assistance. I went to the social services, but I didn't have time to go through all the paperwork because I had to be back at the telephone by a certain time to receive the call for the 'interview'. I told the caseworker I had to leave because I was expecting a call from the White House. He looked at me funny, and told me to come back when I was ready. He said he wouldn't have any problems obtaining assistance for me."

"How did you discover the ozone connection with combustion?"

"It was the smell. The smell of a new furnace burning near the incident. The smell of lightning. The left hand of God. The frozen star we all carry to our sleep."

"I smell a schizo," Misty whispered to Charley. "Let's go?"

"Hey Soddy, we gotta go, man, Dan, er... Dangerous Dan has got the car running good and the snow has stopped." Thanks a lot for all the good things. Keep in touch-yeah?"

Soddy crumbled his bread and watched the taillights wizen down the hill.

BATTERED NOVA, BIRCH AND CALICO

Every winter a stray cat comes around or is dropped off. This winter it was a little calico which had to find a family quick. It made friends with Charley who tucked it in his down-filled vest and gave it some of his hamburger. Today's task was to get a chain saw running. They had to retrieve a chainsaw which was lent to Harry. Harry the Financier, friend of a famous sneak, alias Chief-Many-Networks, a.k.a. The "Cockroach," because he usually came out at night. He became the father figure to Fuzzy, who was part Indian and perused weather and electricity. Dangerous Dan had been into guns that winter. He never shot anything, but liked to see the holes a bullet would make in various objects. On occasion he would try to shoot Fuzzy-at Fuzzy's request, in order to appease or settle bets on Fuzzy's rainmaking abilities and other spells that went awry.

They walked down the village street exchanging salutations. A faint smell of old damp moldings in the windows of houses near the sidewalk slid along the elmsmoke and collided with a bit of air, rising from a swelling cesspool. They walked around a big building which was surrounded by cars with their fronts, or rears, resting on cement blocks or on parts of old stoves, like helpless bugs decaying, flipped off a grid. Most had been cannibalized for parts. None was running.

"Hey, Harry!" They pounded on the door. Nothing. They pounded again. "Hey, Harry!"

"Yeah?"

"It's me," Charley, "with Dangerous Dan and Fuzzy."

"Wait a minute."

The voice sounded illegal; a speakeasy voice amplified through illicit substances, antiques, gold watches and stuffed animals before it could wheeze itself to the door.

"C'min."

They followed Harry in and sat in a den-like room with racks of guns filling the upper part of the walls.

"What are all these guns for?" Dan asked.

"I like 'em. I like the looks of them," Harry said, hinting that he'd like to say a lot more about them.

"What's that one over there standing in the corner?"

Harry walked over and removed the clip. "This here's my carbine...BUDDY. This is what the officers use. It's short-barreled. This is an extra long clip. People know I have a lot of valuables here, so I have to protect them. They go up in value...these guns are worth a LOT of money...BUD-DY. Besides, if things keep going like they are, you'll need 'em. Things are gonna git a lot worse, man. They'll start coming up from the cities looting and stealing. I'll be ready for 'em. You wait...things are gonna get worse. These guns...they'll be worth barter. I got ammunition. I got whole cartons full. That's gonna be the trade. Money won't be any good. Only like ammunition... tools...I can get along for three winters. I'm telling ya...it's gonna get bad. I mean, I can go out and earn a living anytime, man...I got skills. I'm the best body man there is. I can rebuild a whole car in one day. Big government's got it where you can't do anything. Big government and oil companies. You wait and see. Everything has got to go back to real value. People are HUNGRY. The cities are going to go, man."

"Are you from here?"

"Long Island. I grew up there. But I'll never go back there. No way. Too many niggers and spics. Too cold for 'em up here. But you watch. The cities...they'll go under."

"Did you have guns when you where a kid?"

"Yeah...I used to have a 22. Me and my buddies on the Island...we'd take an old Model T and tie it to a stake in the ground...anchor it good on something, then we'd put out the throttle and tie the steering wheel so's it'd go around in a circle. Then we'd shoot it full of holes."

Harry insisted they have a beer because he wanted to talk. His younger apprentices came in. They would find him rare watches, turtle totems, old girly magazines, smoke, pills, Persian rugs, ammunition, dried food, stove wood, you name it—but they couldn't have beer for nothing. Charley or Dangerous Dan could. He first had to tell his apprentices what he had to do to make money, and how he made it when he was their age. Then maybe...maybe they deserved a beer—if they "turned up" something for him. Thieves and cheats OK, but freeloaders—that's something else.

"You watch him while I go to the refrigerator and get some beer." He pointed to Jesus who seemed to take it all in stride.

"There's not many of them up here. Too cold for them. But he's good. He knows I'm not prejudiced."

He ordered one of them to get some more wood for the stove. Each had definite duties that evolved from Harry's "school." The kitchen counter was covered with wrenches, grinders, oilcans, etc. Outside the window, the snow was blowing off the tops of car bodies. The best body and fender man in the country didn't have a complete car to go anywhere. Not that he needed to. He would spend months, sometimes a whole winter and summer inside watching wrestling on T.V. while they came to him. A gold watch, a T.V. set, an antique doll, a stuffed animal, a carved Indian-the room filled. Guns and gold watches were the primary items. Next came wood.

"My friend Dangerous Dan wants to write some poetry," Charley said to Harry. "He wants to stay at Ben's farm for a while."

"Yeah...he lives up at that place? I saw a bear up there not long ago. There's plenty of deer up there. I go hunting up there. Poetry. Huh. I don't like any of it. It's all crazy shit to me. He lives up there with those queers?

"No one's up there now, except Mantra Chickie."

"Nah..she's shackin' with Soddy."

"They'd better have some wood in up there. A storm's on the way. I haven't seen any of them this winter. That one with the long beard who used to come down here screaming about Fascism...and the other one with hair down to his ass...I haven't seen for a while. The one with long hair came down here and started screaming for everyone to stop drinking beer. He was yelling at the farmers on how to plant crops. They think he's psycho. If you look at them wrong they go off screaming about Fascism. They come around in the summer and deliver free cow shit for people's gardens. But no one wants it. There's enough shit washes down from those pastures to grow anything. You can hear him screamin' about the government and fascists. They say he's got connections, though. They say he's got money. He knows people in high places."

A knock on the door and two men stepped in from the winding path through cannibalized car bodies. They stamped the snow off their boots and rubbed their hands over the stove.

"What you got?" Asked Harry.

"I have one here. A real gold one."

They sat around the table. Harry ran his hand around the brim of his hat. He was never seen without his greasy cowboy hat that was a little too small for his head. Especially this night...he wore a bandage wrapped around his head with the hat perched on top.

"Wha'd you do to your head?" Charley asked.

"I ran into Bob, the other morning about 2 a.m."

"What'y mean you ran into him?"

"Well he ran into me. You know where that road comes off the old turnpike into town? He came right over the hill and crashed into our Nova. I just about froze before they got me to the hospital. They sewed up my head." Harry had stitches in his hat in the same pattern as the stitches in his head. "I'm going to get a LOT of money out his insurance company on this one," he said as he put a pot of water on the stove.

"How could you have run into him at that time?" Charley asked. "No one's out on the road around here at that hour. Were you drinking?"

"I don't know how it happened. All I know is that his car came up over the hill and ran right into my Nova. I'll get some money out of this...you wait and see. Though money ain't worth nothin' now. I'll buy watches. I'm looking for a watch that was made around here. I think I know where to find it. It costs a LOT of money. But I can buy it. You'll see. We're going into a depression. Money isn't worth anything. Only guns, ammunition, gold...and food." He pulled out his billfold stuffed with large bills...and gave Jesus some money to get a sixpack. "...And make sure you bring me the change."

He dipped out some spaghetti and started eating it with his pocketknife.

"I don't even have a fork. But I got a billfold full of money."

"What are you eating?" Someone asked.

"Spaghetti."

"Just spaghetti! Are you in training for the depression?"

"I'm tellin' ya. It's gonna get bad. They ain't doin' nothin' about it. People can't pay these taxes. They pay more now, accordingly, per person, than when the kings collected from the serfs. But here you won't see it so bad. This place has always been depressed. It won't make any difference here."

Someone passed around a big box of weed.

"Here...someone roll some joints," he said fingering the weed. "What the hell's this?" One said rolling a soft, brown ball in his fingers.

"I don't know," Fuzzy said. "I thought it was hash and ate some."

One of the men with the watches started laughing and held the substance between his fingers. "Hell, these are rabbit turds!"

"Rabbit turds!" Spat Fuzzy. "No wonder my ears have been feeling fuzzy!"

"Well, someone gave it to me," Harry said sheepishly. "They had it in a big box with rabbits. Well, here's some home grown," said Harry. "I don't smoke it much. I like my beer. You know where this came from?" He grinned slyly. "I found this along the running board of my car before Bob ran into me. I'm not kidding. It had been growing in it all summer while the car was on blocks in the shop. I didn't discover it until I put the car on the road. I had a whole plant in the dirt inside the door."

Charley moved over to the ancient bay window where layers of paint had sculpted the angles of the moldings much like snow itself. The purple wind cut through the cracks reminding him of the Nor'easterly which had its fury waiting at the window, uncivilized, wild-eyed, like a Paint horse wanting full lope.

Harry turned to Dangerous Dan. "So you came up from the city? You need some money? What can you do. Me, I'm a body man. I got all the tools I need right in the next room. I own this whole building. When I get finished with this I'll have something. I'm refinishing the whole building, Bud-dy, from top to bottom."

"Well, I don't do much of anything right now," replied Dangerous Dan. "I work slow. I turn wrenches. I rest easy. I keep quiet. I came from a long line of bottom people. I'm the bottom line, you might say. There are not many changes in my life. I've made several mistakes. Once you get older there's not much for you these days. I wish I could have worked like you did in the 50's. Those were good times. Now I know the scam that's being run. I know there's not much out there for a young person. Even with college. That's the only chance, but even that ain't as good as it used to be. The world caught up with my generation. We have to pay the tab to be the same as those other countries that didn't make it. We're like little countries that can't make it for ourselves. The old big company store routine. We have to buy in to the big scam no matter what. We have to get used to poverty. If you haven't built up something in this little life, or have something laid on ya from the old folks at home, there's no way to get it now. Oh I've written down a few songs...I could go back and sing them like I got something to say...but you know how that is. No one wants to hear a loser. I got a few bucks for my work but I blew it all at the track. Chance itself was better for me than nothing. And what is there, really? Maybe I like it here. Maybe I just want to be a Townie. Maybe flip some burgers at the local pub, write a few songs, drink some beer, write some poems, and wait to die. What's it to you? But everyone wants their say. And what is mine? The wind is full of voices, and it keeps pressing, you know. Pressing all the time; we all want to be heard, but I can't tell you how awful it is to try to catch some piece of voice and present it for your own. But it's not enough just to be heard; we want more power. If our words give us power, then we become politicians; we have to please our constituencies. Then power strips all truth and nobility from life. It makes wars, misery, nuclear reactors, and all evils associated with life. It's all accumulated at another's expense and becomes the energy that consumes us all; we consume the same waste that eats silently of our very lives. We are contaminated. Forever. No one knows what we're here for. It's dark."

Harry shook his head grievously. "Hey, Charley, what's the snow doing out there?"

Charley jerked on the bottom of the window blind...and let go. It raised an inch. Angrily he tugged at it again and let go. It raised a couple of inches. He repeated the process. It netted an inch and a half. He threw the blind over his back; it came off the brackets and slid down him in a worthless sheet, the brackets dangled loosely from the assorted nail holes of past years. "I'm sorry about the blind," he said to Harry.

"Hey," Harry answered, "whad'y I care? Look, the sun has just peeked outa the clouds. It might get up to freezing today. Tell you what...that snow ain't too deep. It'd be a good day to get some wood. I'll make a deal with ya. I might buy the gold watch later, but right now I'll give you that chain saw to help bring this old guy I know some wood. He's got something I been wantin', and he'll only trade for wood. He wants to put up some wood now to cure it for next season. He's particular. Wants it all cut and stacked in an exact cord. If the log is bigger around than a football he wants it split in two. Wants apple; maple; white birch...no elm."

"I burn elm. Burns good," said Charley. "Hard elm'll burn all night. A glowing charcoal log'll be there the next morning...the same shape only shrunk down. It burns hotter than they say. I like to put in some big elm knots overnight. Put 'em on top of a nice hot oak or ash fire. It keeps things toasty. Nothing wrong with elm."

"Well, he says it don't split good, and he likes it split down for handling and burning. Anyways, he's got something I want. I ain't saying what, yet. But it's hard to come by. I'll tell you what I'll do. You help me get this cord of wood together, and I'll give you this chain saw, or you can have a share in what he trades me. You can look at it before you make up your mind. Dangerous Dan will help us."

"I don't know," said Dangerous Dan, "I've never cut wood before. Sounds like a lot of work."

"Nothin' to it," said Harry, "I know this guy who has a contract on state land. He didn't get it all cut out before the weather got too bad. He said I could have it. I know his mark. It would be easy to get it out now. The snow's not too deep. He told this friend of mine anyone could have it; whoever got it out before the contract expired."

Such as it was in all Harry's deals. He liked to set up situation with as many variables as possible to see what would come of it to his advantage. The more complex the dealings, the better. What else to do but stir up smoldering risks, Chief Many Networks? He always maintained a straight and narrow course, not wanting to be thought of as someone who would take advantage of another, but his "caveat emptor" was very avaricious; the path he trod a bit too shady, his countenance, a weed growing in a garden.

"I don't have a chain to fit this saw," Charley said.

"Tell you what I'll do," Harry offered. "It so happens I have this other chain saw. It's a good one. It's small...but good for limbing. You gotta watch these small ones, though...a branch will snap back and throw it right onto you. They just took someone to the hospital that other day with his face and shoulder cut. A branch got him. You gotta watch those branches."

"Yeah, that's why I like my big saw," Charley added. "Ain't no one gonna be liftin' that sucker very high. You can set it right down on the wood. It'll set there and go right through anything."

"How we gonna draw the wood?" Harry asked.

"We can use the Behemoth, the 4-by," said Charley. "You'll have to cut him in on the deal somehow. You could throw a little wood his way. He needs some. He burns it wet. His 'Jimmy' will haul a cord. It's got a 400 in it. It'll haul anything you put on it. It's old, but you can't stop it. It's a crew-cab too. It's got a 4-wheel and a winch. We can get up the mountain in that. Hell yes! It can draw a cord of wood."

"Good," said Fuzzy. "I'll get my Nova running. It just needs some gas in it. Harry, you can come with me and take the chain saw to this guy I know who repairs them. He'll tell you what it's worth. It's a good deal. I ain't cheatin' ya. I'll pay for the plug it needs. It shouldn't need anything else. He might have to set the carburetor a little."

Harry and Fuzzy set to work on the best Nova with the unmatched fenders. After tinkering with it, they went to get the saw fixed. As they approached the driveway, a German shepherd tugged on a chain wrapped around a 50 gallon oil drum. Greasy signs of trade-name parts shingled and patched the tarpaper house. From behind a bench heaped with old parts, advanced a man whose face held no expression whatsoever.

"Hi," greeted Fuzzy. "Me and my friend here was wondering if you had time to look at this saw. It needs a plug, and maybe a carburetor adjustment. It runs a little rough, feels like it chokes out."

The man, unmoved by the diagnosis, walked wearily towards Harry and Fuzzy. The German shepherd bared its teeth and strained and growled. "It'll cost ya," said the man, looking down at the dog. "Don't pay him no mind. He won't bite yuh." The man took the chain saw from Harry, with an arm as hard as a tree limb, and yanked the cord ferociously. The man had on a short sleeve shirt torn away at the buttons. His face was etched with hate and misery. His German shepherd looked at him loyally, and at no one else. The furrows in his face were of an abandoned field, once plowed, then left to erode, a field that could have remained a meadow that nature would not leave so harsh an imprint. He was bent from labor. His dreams as cold as the propane in the tanks leaning against his shed.

"It needs a needle valve," he said.

Fuzzy paid cash for the repairs, and they drove toward the woods.

"Hey," he said to Harry, "I gotta calico worth some money."

"Wot's a calico?"

"A cat."

"Hmmfh. How can a cat be worth money? They're nothing but moochers. I don't like cats."

"It's a Male."

"So?"

"A male calico. It's rare. I'll show you. I have this newspaper clipping; wait 'til we get back to your place. These cats bring thousands of dollars for genetic research, or from people who collect them. It's worth a lot of money."

"Hmmf," said Harry as they approached the woods. There they met Dangerous Dan and Charley who had taken their chain saw apart.

"What's happening?" Asked Fuzzy.

"I've got to put this chain back on the sprocket," said Charley.

"Hey, look at that white birch," said Harry. "I could really use that. Birch burns good."

"It isn't marked."

"Yeah but look. It needs trimming out. It's blocking the growth of those saplings. Any way, I marked them for the forestry when I was working on a CETA job marking trees."

"You were high when you marked up here, huh Harry?"

"We'd better get started. Not much daylight left."

They cut for a few hours, trimmed and threw the firewood onto the truck, then sat down to finish off another six-pack.

"Wheh, this is hard, back killing work," said Fuzzy.

"Hell, I can fill that whole truck, myself," said Harry. "In no more time than we've all spent. You don't know work."

"Hey, about the watch, you think you want it?"

"I have to think about it. It has Ginny markings on it. I don't like Ginny watches. I might be interested in those cats though, if you can show me that stuff about them."

"Sure, I can show you when we get back."

"I'd sure like to have that tree," Fuzzy said, eyeing the white birch. "It's just the right size to split easy. I tell you what I'll do. You help me take that birch, and I'll consider buying yer calco. What is it? Cal..cal.."

"Calico. All right. Let's go. But if we get caught, it's your tree."

"Don't worry, they ain't no rangers up here this time of year."

Charley looked at the tree. He felt its soft white skin and looked up at its majestic form and color against the green pine and barren branches of the dark maples.

"This is the most perfectly shaped tree I've ever seen."

"Yeah, it's just the right size for firewood. I'll notch it for you. We're going to have to notch it on this side so it'll go between that maple and the pines."

"But then it'll be falling downhill. It'll be harder to draw out."

"We can pull it out with the winch."

"OK, but you still have to clear those saplings."

"It'll take them with it. You'll see. I'll notch it so it'll go between them. We don't have to take them out. It'll clear them."

He began sawing into the beautiful trunk. He sawed a notch and knocked it out. Harry looked at it. It's sap ran. It was all wet inside. It's history of a good life was recorded in its perfect rings.

"OK, you can take it down with this saw," Fuzzy instructed Charley.

Charley began to saw as they all watched for the fall. His saw dug into the soft wet skin as he tried to think of some kind of prayer to offer, above the terrible sound of the saw. It's mechanical teeth grabbed at the living tree and spewed it out on linear plane across a mechanical universe like an analog of Western thought. The ring of years were circled deep in the tree's wounded history. He became dizzy with power and clinched his teeth. The tree swayed, but refused to fall. He took his saw out of the gash and pushed on the tree. It remained upright in defiance. Charley looked at the weight distribution of its upper branches. It might not fall as planned. He planned for an escape. He cleared a path just in case and then went back to cutting. The others looked toward the top of the tree, aligning their own limbs with the angles of their speculation. Each had points of variation on how it would fall. But it was Charley's tree now; he was making the cut. He pushed the saw back and forth as he cut. The tree didn't move. He began to respect the tree, but it was too late. Over half its trunk was cut out. An irreversible notch was cut in nature, in life. Nothing to do now but destroy it. He began to worry as he cut. It must have had less than a half inch left in the center of its trunk. The tree then seemed to give out a vast, cracking, silent ache as it began wobbling. It was severed now, dizzy. What little bit left to cut would easily break. Still, there was no indication of its direction of fall. Charley made a fast cut and stepped back. The great birch swayed, leaned gently in a great hush of the forest, and fell in the soft pine branches. The other trees caught its fall as it leaned against its own firm trunk, squeezing its soft skin as its sap ran. The pressure of its wedge in this position was much greater than when it stood erect. The men sighed and cussed. It was harder than ever to cut a leaning tree. They began notching and cutting and trying to get it to fall. They cut another section and it fell a little more wedging itself again between the trees holding it and its own trunk. There wasn't much daylight left. They worked fast. As much time and energy was now spent as was needed to cut down several trees. The birch fought up to the last cut. It had now wedged itself between another tree and the ground. Each cut was a new problem. The tree was still trying to stand, truncated, against each section cut away. With only a few more feet left, the men worked feverishly. In the fall of its last section it hit a maple branch which broke and landed on the roof of Fuzzy's Nova with a resounding bang.

"Look out," Fuzzy cried as it came down. "Oh no! Not my car!"

They stopped cutting and looked at the damage while tipping their bottles for the last drop.

The white birch was on the ground ready to be trimmed and quartered. They began cutting it up in small pieces. The pieces of its white limbs lay about on the forest floor like shattered skeleton on a white, green, and brown blanket. Harry took the smaller saw and made a cut on one of its branches which was bent like a bow under another piece. As it was cut loose it pushed the saw back into Harry's face gashing his cheek.

"Harry's been hurt!"

They stopped cutting and carried Harry to the truck. Charley looked at the gash and could see a speck of white cheekbone.

"We have to get him to the hospital."

Charley got the truck started as Fuzzy helped Harry into the cab. He drove as fast as he could down the mountain. They came upon Mantra's Jeep which was blocking the road. Mantra was in the cab meditating.

"Mantra, what the hell are you doing? We got to get past. Harry's had an accident."

"Yeah...I was going up to Ben's farm and ran out of gas," she said passively.

"Look, we have to get the truck over so's we can get by. We'll have to push you!"

"Fuzzy, you get in and guide her truck."

They pushed it over, and it went into a ditch.

"Sorry," Fuzzy said, "but this is an emergency. They'll be some other guys on their way down, they'll help you." As they left, Mantra Woman was trying to sit upright, crosslegged on the truck seat which was leaning into the ditch.

Harry got his cut sewed up and went back to his place. Dangerous Dan went by to see him and offered him some wood.

"Thanks, thanks. I may need some. I have some new additions to the family."

"Oh yeah! What do you mean?"

"Cats. Fuzzy gave me some real cute calico kittens. Said he hated cats."

ONCE THE MILERMORE SANG

Summer came and went. Misty broke the onion tops in the garden and ran in a field of dandelions. Dangerous Dan was busy putting his car on the road, which meant in these parts that everything had to be repaired. Everything rusts or rots so quickly that summertime was always too short to get everything done. Charley couldn't keep up with his projects. Before one was complete, another grew from it, and the original one was left undone. By now, Dangerous Dan was doing some part-time social work. He was on the case of a woman who had been left by a man who had followed a fabulous heron. He had asked Mary to come with him because the woman had a heavy sexual appetite for him. She also wanted him to fix her car, because her old man didn't fix anything. All he did was sell nightcrawlers. He had been friends with the man who left her to follow the noon-bird, or heron.

"C'min."

The doorknob came off in his hand.

"Damn thing. Won't stay on. The shaft's too long for the hole. They say they were good craftsmen, but they weren't.

Weren't any better'n me. Hell, when I'se ten, my old man died and left me the man of the house."

"Whay'd ya do with him?"

"Doan pay no tenshun to her, she crazy."

"Tha's why you come here. You from the county?"

A faint smell of dry rot from the windowsill rose with the elmsmoke and sewer gas from a swelling cesspool.

"Tell me how you've been feeling, ma'm, while I fill out these papers."

"Very peaceful. There's a lot more to it than we realize. Although I liked it up there with the others in the ward. Boy, could Johnny polka! I like to be home better. Don't that take the cake? So I catch myself using dated expressions like that, and it gives me hovering wing feelings and the days go by in transparencies. But I have to live here even though I'm educated I still show love for the other man. I came from a good home. I used to listen to Handel's Ode to St. Cecilia all day long, I can hear the words now. It was about a dandelion which went, 'Joyous supernal it sits on a weed. Oh...Oh....OH! Joyous supernal it sits on a weed.'" I used to play it like my three-fingered exercise."

"Can you tell me how it made you feel?"

"My exercise!"

"No, the music."

"His music made me feel like if a wild animal or a snake were to bite me, I could take care of it and not give it infection. I came from a nice home. Before eating my oldest sister Amy always said grace. My uncle would be very meticulous though he wouldn't come on a white horse or a white suit. I had class, but the result of endless leisure is usually guilt and worthlessness, and with luck, a little porcelain. So I married a local mechanic who couldn't even keep the car running. A lot of people have not experienced living with someone by themselves."

I'm a mechanic too," said Dangerous Dan.

Parts of old cars, cannibalized, rested on cement blocks under the snow.

"And he...he ran off after that damn bird. I saw it once, rising just above the road, like a big bomber. Its wings were as wide as our car, then it barely got enough height to fly into the woods. Its head and neck were like a prehistoric bird."

"I still hear it whispering sometimes at noon."

"He thinks he does. What he hears is the village noon whistle down the valley. They're rather proud of their whistle."

"Ask her. She knows it brings messages. Just ask her. It portends!"

She said she looked into the sky last night and that there's a lot more to it than we realize. She said she saw a king with a tall hat sitting on a receding spiral. She saw geometrical shapes zoom larger and smaller without changing their original shape. She said they come from outer spheres and go beneath the skin," her old man said.

"What kind of shapes?"

"Triangles on top of each other."

"One more thing while I have my clipboard handy. Has she been having any trouble with her memory?"

"I can't remember any."

"What is this bird? Do you know about this bird, Mary?" Mary crossed her hands and forearms deep between her legs and crossed her thighs forcefully as she pulled her arms up with a look of pleasure. She began to appear beautiful under her long coarse red hair. You could almost visualize the pleasant mound under the fly of her patched levis."

"My uncle followed the bird. He said it belonged out west, that it wanted to go back to its mountains. Soddy said it's the Clew-bird. It sticks its bill in the ground and whistles loud through its rectum. Some fishermen call it the milermore because its whistle can be heard along ways. He said this one was a variety known as the noon-bird that whistles at high noon."

"What was the man's name who followed the bird?" Dangerous Dan picked up his clipboard.

"Shjaket, Shajaket Dugan," she replied.

"What kind of a name is Shjaket, Shajket?

"Some say he was a Holy Man."

"Wad he look like?"

"The Iahtola."

"Khomanl?"

"Just the one."

"This has given me a clue!" Said Dangerous Dan. "I saw a guy named Dugan in the city, when we left. He was looked like a Bowery Bum. Mary, what if I told you that I had found your uncle?"

"Oh, I'd want to see him!"

"Then we'll go back to the city and find him."

It was summertime when Charley drove Dangerous Dan and Mary down the mountain trail again. They saw the pieces of the birch still strewn about as they had left them. Some were beginning to get soft with mulch on their underside. They drove past a little blue train stopped in a valley at the end of a large field of dandelions.

"Ah...where else could you see this," Charley said.

When they went past Harry's, Harry was sitting on his porch.

"Hi, Harry!"

"Hey, good to see you both, how's it going?"

"Fine. How's yourself?"

"Oh I'm fine, considering," he looked about and wiggled his eyebrows. "Anyway it's a place to be. I can leave anytime I'm ready. I'm trying to work into a job at construction..Things ain't so bad."

"Where you two going?"

"We're leaving town."

"You be back?"

"You know we will. Let me see your cheek. Hell you can hardly tell there's a scar there."

"Yeah...it's my birchmark," Harry said foolishly. "Hey, have you seen Fuzzy lately?"

"Yeah, I went by his place the other night. He was sitting in his rocker drinking beer. Had his stereo going full blast listening to Neil Diamond. He made me listen a while...saying he's the greatest singer in the world."

"Hey, Dangerous Dan wrote a poem for him. Maybe you can give it to him next time you see him."

"Sure I'd be glad to. Can I see it?"

"Sure. I'll even read it for you. I called it 'Lines of Sunset'. It has something to do with the snow that fell that night and maybe the lines and angles, I don't know. Tell him if he can't understand it, don't worry, I can't either."

The snow came
   rolled its armies
   against the lines
   of most resistance
Made a silent order
   to powder the chaos
   smiled softly
   in white coffin

The snow came
   fell like a visit
   of souls
   distilled from stars
Its numbers like
   old lace floating on the grass
The snow came
   covered the dirt
   and the beer cans
   the new smelling sawdust
The snow came
   leaked through the sneakers of children
   on the way to school
   or violin lessons
The snow came
   to all new life of the world
   settled under the iron
   as well as the wound
Though fields now plowed may
   not be plowed this spring.

"Well, I think it's great. After a few weeks of getting the caddy revived they set out for the city. It was a sunny day along the Hudson and the caddy was looking fine. By the time they got to the last rest stop it was raining.

"I hungry," Mary said. "I could eat a weiner."

"I think I'll have a hot dog," said Dangerous Dan. "There's not much they can do to a hot dog at these places.'

"That sounds cool. Make it two."

The picture of roasted weiners turning in Dangerous Dan's mind made him think of the races. "Ah this reminds me of the track, Secretariat and Riva Ridge, neck and neck. I can see them now. Look at them both set down their left forelegs! You have to develop your eye. It takes years of watching. There they go, about one stride every 43 hundredths of a second. Zip! Zip! Zip! Look at that shit! They're in sync; they're both about to set down their left forelegs simultaneously...but wait ! . Secretariat's RIGHT foreleg, which is you know... the last leg to touch down... is just about to leave the ground! Look at Riva Ridge's right foreleg- not yet in midstride, Secretariat's pace- even spokes. Not much extension there, sweetheart, he ain't spending much time on the ground."

Ah! civilization, we're close enough to the city. I'll get a N.Y.C. hot dog, he thought out loud.

He noticed the whole place was run by Haitians. The cook, the dishwasher, the bus boys. Everyone! He thought it strange since this was part of the New York State Throughway.

The cashier collected the money. The waiter put two nuked prepackaged hotdogs on the counter. Dangerous Dan and Mary opened them curiously.

"Hey this won't do," Dangerous Dan told the counter person. "This hot dog is green."

"You'll have to see the manager."

"Call the manager!"

One of the Haitians disappeared behind a swinging door. Out came another, in a business coat over white pants looking much like the first one.

"I'm not going to eat this. I want my money back."

The Haitians removed their aprons, put down their mops and conferred about the refund."

"You can have your money back."

"I want her's too."

"You trying to lose customers!"

"No! I'm trying to keep my friend from getting sick."

The Haitians reluctantly returned the money. Dangerous Dan and Mary got in the Caddy and drove into the bowels Manhattan. The tranny was making a noise and Dan crawled under the Caddy, oblivious to the slim that ran down the gutter. He twisted the drive shaft with his hand.

"H'mmm" well this feels O.K." You now I used to work on Jaguars. They all have a leak in the oil pan. Can you imagine that?"

Dan and Charley sat on a warm grate on Prince St. and began watching a kid do tricks with a little cardboard cutout. It was a simple thing. The kid looked like he might have been working his way through Columbia U. He had a bag of the little cardboard cutout figures. As if by magic the figure would obey him when he told it to lie down, or take a bow, Etc. It appeared to work magic. A Hispanic gut became hypnotized and soon grimaced over not knowing how the trick was done. Its got to have strings attached. The kid waved his hand above the figure...no strings. This went on for hours. Crowds came and went. It only cost $5.00 to buy the figure with instructions. Though that was cheap, no one wanted to be chumped, so it kept going and going.

Dan was coughing and offered a drink from his bottle to Charley, who declined.

"What's a matter, you afraid of the virus?"

"No, Dan, though I know you look like a hippy and hippies used to share everything and you're too young to know this, but you instinctively have all the traits of a hippy. In Fact, you are the last young hippy, who was never a hippy. Besides, it is my hypothesis that a virus, take the T-4 for instance, really follows sound. So one is more in danger of catching a virus through one's ears than through that bottle of French wine, which, by the way is the worst I've drunk. French Drano."

"Well how does this Virus get into your ear?"

"Well, that's a long story, Danny, and I'm getting tired, and we haven't figured out this kid's trick.

Do you believe in magic? Ah That's it. I've been trying to think of that for days, listening to it on the radio when we were moving to Baltimore. The Hot Chocolates. Of course! Now you see Dan, The virus rides the vibes which of course goes at a speed that cuts time. But never mind that now. That's volumetric space, from the gnomon again. I have sat on the throne of Osiris and know the Directions...and none of us can escape Directions, can we Dan? The big D. Well, its directions and yours and mine all twist in that old helix, just twisting the night away, that was Chubby Checker, you don't remember him, took his name from Fats Domino, long after I used to groove with Fats out at de Mambo Club, pronounced as Ma'am. De Ma'am Bo. Ah so long ago. But you see there's a flutter in the long chain of DNA. That's like dream. That's where the Magic comes in. Invisible nonsense junk interrupts the code and all of a sudden... an aberration in the strand. Every living thing has and aberration in the strand, the invisible thread that winds and unwinds us forever. When the code flutters, the dream stuff sputters. If that virus's flutter comes in when your is flutter...watch out. That's when you catch it. You catch it in the code, catch a cold in the code. I want to sleep on this concrete and think of San Francisco in 1963. You weren't born yet, but something happened. Just like the string on that little cutout is curved in space. The star appears to be here. The star is really here, and that dent becomes the curve that eternally returns to its beginnings. That crossed the orbit in 1963, I'm sorry for these facts, Max, but there are little variations in the elliptical path. All time is not the same, even though our watches tick the same."

Charles Plymell Selected Bibliography

Selections. Privately printed, 1960. Poems.

(Editor) Roxie Powell. Dreams of Straw. Privately printed, 1963. Poems.

Apocalypse Rose. With introduction by Allen Ginsberg. Dave Haselwood Books, 1966. Poems.

Neon Poems. Atom Mind Publications, 1970.

The Last of the Moccasins. City Lights Books, 1971. Novel. Published as Moccasins Ein Beat-Kaleidoskop in Austria by Euopaverlag, 1980.

Over The Stage of Kansas. Telephone Books, 1973. Poems.

The Trashing of America: Phase 1. The Unspeakable Visions of the Individual, 1973. Poems.

The Trashing of America. Kulchur Foundation, 1975. Poems.

Are You A Kid? Cherry Valley Editions, 1977. Poems.

Blue Orchid Numero Uno. Telephone Books, 1977. Poems.

In Memory of My Father. Cherry Valley Editions, 1981. Poems.

Panik in Dodge City. Expanded Media Editions, 1981. Poems.

Forever Wider: Poems New and Selected, 1954-1984. Scarecrow Press, 1985.

The Harder They Come. Immediate Editions, 1985. Interview.

Was Poe Afraid? Bogg Publications, 1989. Poems.

Journals From Lysidia. Synaesthesia Press, 1999. Essay.

Publisher and Printer

1959 - Poets' Corner, publisher
1959 - Mikrokosmos, publisher
1963 - NOW, publisher
1964 - NOW NOW, publisher
1965 - NOW NOW NOW, publisher
1967 - Bulletin From Nothing, printer
1967 - The Last Times, editor and publisher
1967 - Zap Comix, Number 1, printer
1967 - Grist magazine, guest editor, publisher
1974 - 1979 Coldspring Journal (co-editor, co-publisher)
1976 - 1981 Northeast Rising Sun (co-editor, co-publisher)

Pamela and Charles Plymell, Cherry Valley, New York, November 1998. After Ray Bremser's memorial service.

A major figure in the history of American contemporary literature and poetry, Charles Plymell was born in Holcomb, Kansas in 1935. An active participant in the small press renaissance throughout the 1960s and 1970s as author, publisher and printer, his work continues to appear in countless literary journals and anthologies today. He lives in Cherry Valley, New York with his wife, Pamela Beach Plymell, and their dog, Be Bop.

Endsheet photos:
1. Charles & Pam Plymell. City Lights, SF, 1966
2. Apocalypse Rose back cover, 1966, Turk St., SF
3. Charles Plymell, Baltimore, 1969
4. Trashing Of America back cover, 1973, Bagby, California